Volume 1

Plants for the Home

John J. Bagnasco

nature life®

McGill/Jensen, Inc.
655 Fairview Ave. No.
St. Paul, Minn. 55104

Plants for the Home

Copyright© 1976 by Nature Life Division, McGill/Jensen, Inc.

ISBN 0-918134-02-1

To my dearest wife,
Shannon

Acknowledgements

I would first like to thank all the indoor plant growers across the country for their enthusiasm and the information they have shared with me on the culture of plants. I would also like to thank the associates with whom I work for their efforts in promoting the entire nursery industry. Recognition should also be given to horticultural instructors in schools all over the world for their efforts to spread information in this rapidly growing field.

I would like to thank my wife, my family, and friends for their influence and support and finally, I would like to thank God for making my life possible and filling it with more blessings than I deserve or could ever imagine.

Contents

Vining Plants for Hanging Baskets

Asparagus Fern
Candle Plant
Creeping Impatiens
English Baby Tears
English Ivy
Flame Violet
German Ivy
Giant White Inch Plant
Golden Pothos
Goldfish Plant
Grape Ivy

Heartleaf Philodendron
Kangaroo Ivy
Lipstick Vine
Piggyback Plant
Purple Heart
Purple Passion Vine
Red Ivy
Satin Pellionia
Spider Plant
Strawberry Begonia
String of Hearts

String of Pearls
Striped Inch Plant
Swedish Ivy
Sweetheart Ivy
Tahitian Bridal Veil
Teddy Bear Vine
Vining Peperomia
Wandering Jew
Wax Ivy
Wax Plant

Ferns and Foliage Plants

Baby's Tears
Bird's Nest Fern
Boston Fern
Buddhist Pine
Button Fern
Chinese Evergreen
Coffee Plant
Dragon Palm
Dumb Cane
Emerald Ripple
Fiddleleaf Fig

Fluffy Ruffles Fern
Green Nephthytis
Holly Fern
Iron Cross Begonia
Maidenhair Fern
Norfolk Island Pine
Parlor Palm
Ponytail Palm
Prayer Plant
Rabbit's Foot Fern
Ribbon Plant

Rubber Plant
Silver Table Fern
Spider Aralia
Split-leaf Philodendron
Staghorn Fern
Tsus-sima Fern
Umbrella Plant
Umbrella Tree
Variegated Pittosporum
Weeping Fig

Cacti and Succulents

Bird Nest Sansevieria
Bishop's Cap
Bunny Ears
Burro's Tail
Christmas Cactus
Elkhorn Cactus
Fishhook Cactus
Golden Barrel Cactus
Golden Stars
Golf Balls
Grafted Cacti

Irish Mittens
Jade Plant
Jelly Beans
Medicine Plant
Old Man Cactus
Ox-tongue
Panda Plant
Paperspine Cactus
Partridge Breast
Peanut Cactus
Peruvian Old Man

Powder Puff
Pregnant Plant
Queen Victoria Agave
Red Flowering Crassula
Snake Plant
Star Cactus
Starfish Cactus
Tiger Jaws
Variegated Century Plant
Zebra Haworthia

Flowering and Colorful Foliage Plants

African Violet
Aluminum Plant
Amaryllis
Angelwing Begonia
Bird of Paradise
Cape Primrose
Christmas Kalanchoe
Crossandra
Crown of Thorns
False Heather
Fancy Leaved Caladium

Flamingo Flower
Freckleface
Gardenia
Gloxinia
Gold Dust Dracaena
Gold-spot Euonymus
Hibiscus
Jerusalem Cherry
Kafir Lily
Miniature Orange
Moon Valley Pilea

Mrs. Henry Cox Geranium
Nerve Plant
Pineapple Plant
Rex Begonia
Shrimp Plant
Silver-Vase Bromeliad
Silver Tree
Variegated Peperomia
Watermelon Peperomia
Zebra Plant

Introduction

On the third day of creation, before any living thing existed on earth, God "brought forth vegetation, plants yielding seed, and fruit trees bearing fruit, with seed in them, after their kind; and God saw that it was good." I feel that man senses a kinship with the plant kingdom that he cannot replace with his own creations. Perhaps, this is a reason for the popularity of house plants. In a sterile atmosphere of steel, glass and brick, a green, growing plant can make the world seem less harsh.

Using a strict definition, there is no such thing as an indoor plant. All plants grow naturally outdoors under environmental conditions which specifically suit each species. The most popular "house plants" are those which a number of people have successfully grown indoors and have proven to be the most adaptable to indoor conditions. Some plants will require more light than others, some more water or humidity, just as in nature they are found growing in the environmental situation that suits each species best.

A large part of the enjoyment of growing plants indoors is in trying to duplicate the environmental conditions in which plants survive and thrive. The satisfaction a person gets from being able to say "I did it," is what indoor plant growing is all about. Likewise, the blame for a plant not performing well must lie solely with its owner. No one else is capable of adjusting indoor conditions.

This book is an attempt to make the reader aware of the basic requirements of the most popular house plants and to provide information on how to adjust home conditions to suit each particular species. I have tried to be clear and concise and present the facts in such a form that they are accessible at a quick glance.

I have also tried to give more than just textbook descriptions and care. I have personally grown and cared for every plant in this book. I have also talked to greenhouse growers all over the country and witnessed their techniques in growing certain species. For the novice, I have tried to give simple explanations of basic horticultural principles, but I have also attempted to include information useful to the experienced indoor gardener.

I sincerely hope that the information in this book is useful in promoting the field of home horticulture and in helping each reader to get more satisfactory results in raising and caring for his house plants.

Soil and Soil Fertility

Soil is a complex mixture of weathered particles of inorganic minerals as well as organic materials which have been added as a result of decaying plant and animal matter. About half of a soil's volume is made up of water and air. Besides storing food and water, soil acts as a supporting medium for plants.

Good commercial soil mixes are available at your neighborhood garden center. Most of these mixes have been sterilized and can be adapted to fit any need. Never use soil from outdoors. The little bit of money you may save will be little consolation when a prized plant is lost to soil-borne insects or diseases.

The following soil amendments can be readily obtained and will allow you to adapt any potting soil to fill your need.

VERMICULITE: this is a very light, mica-like mineral which has been expanded by extremely high heat. Its porosity allows it to hold water like a sponge, but it will also improve the drainage of heavy soils. Because it is a sterile medium, it is often used to start seeds or root cuttings.

PERLITE: a white, sterile medium which has been produced from the heat explosion of volcanic rock. Its rough edges hold water, but not as long as vermiculite. Thus, perlite is a good addition to the soil mix of plants that prefer to be kept on the dry side. It also provides a good rooting medium for succulent stems which tend to rot if given too much moisture.

SAND: is finely ground particles of stone, mostly quartz. Coarse sand greatly improves the drainage of any soil mix and is a necessary component of a cactus mix. It is also an excellent rooting medium.

LEAF MOLD: partially decayed leaves, usually oak. This is one of the best sources of organic material. Leaf mold improves the quality and fertility of the soil.

HUMUS: decayed vegetation which aids in the absorption of water by the soil. Humus is helpful in improving soil structure.

PEAT MOSS: the decomposing remains of plants. Sphagnum peat moss is by far the best type of peat, since it resists further decomposition. Peat has good water retaining properties and helps lighten soil texture.

FERTILIZATION is a subject that is often misunderstood. Often a well-meaning plant enthusiast will rush to give an ailing plant a quick dose of fertilizer. But actually, lack of plant food is rarely the cause of a plant looking poorly. The usual reasons are inadequate light or improper watering or possibly a pest problem. However, proper feeding is important.

There are many good house plant foods on the market. The three numbers on each package (for example — 5-10-5) represent the percentages of nitrogen (N), phosphorous (P), and potassium (K) in the fertilizer.* These three elements are the primary nutrients needed for plant growth.

Nitrogen is the element which is most important to leaf and stem growth. Too high a nitrogen level under low light conditions will cause rapid, but weak and leggy plant growth.

Phosphorous is used in root development and flower production. Fruiting and flowering plants should be fertilized with a plant food that is high in phosphorous.

The third primary element is potassium. This nutrient helps to build disease resistance in plants. Potassium also affects flowering, fruiting, and stem strength.

All good house plant foods will contain an ample amount of the above elements. However, more important than the type of fertilizer used, is knowing how often to feed your plants.

Plants which are actively growing during the spring and summer months, will probably benefit from a monthly feeding. During the winter, many plants slow down their growth rate or actually go dormant. Fertilization should be lessened or discontinued during slow growth periods.

The choice and variety of house plant foods is seemingly endless. There are powders, liquids and tablets. Fast-release and slow-release foods; organic and inorganic fertilizers; foods to be used monthly, and foods to be used at each watering. The indoor gardener must decide through experience which food is the best for his plants.

There is one group of plants where the choice of fertilizers is important. These are the "acid-loving" plants which include such members as azaleas, gardenias, camellias, and all citrus plants. These plants need an acid-type fertilizer which should be available from your local garden center.

Improper fertilizing techniques can spell disaster for the home horticulturalist, but proper fertilizing will produce vigorous growth. A well-fertilized plant will exhibit healthy-looking leaves with strong, brilliant colors and will be a specimen of which its owner can be proud.

*The second and third numbers actually stand for the percents of phosphoric acid (P_2O_5) and potash (K_2O) present in the fertilizer.

Pest Problems

Most indoor gardeners realize that warm temperatures coupled with low humidities provide less than ideal growing conditions for tropical plants. What many plant enthusiasts fail to remember is that these common indoor conditions are ideal for many pests that plague plants in the home. Without the presence of their natural enemies, insect pests quickly build up to proportions that will destroy a valued house plant.

For the indoor gardener, insect control is a continuing process. A plant that has been thriving in the same location for years, may suddenly begin to yellow, droop, or look less than healthy. Close inspection will reveal an overpopulation of insect pests that could have been avoided with simple precautionary steps.

Before any new plant is to be added to a collection, it should be isolated for a two week period. Before its quarantine is lifted, the undersides of the leaves should be checked thoroughly for any signs of trouble. The younger leaves at the growing tips of plants are especially vulnerable to attack and should be viewed closely. Even after the plant has been added to a collection it should be checked with all the other plants on a regular basis for problem signs.

Prevention is the best possible method of pest control. The life cycles of insects are very complex and chemical control may be ineffective once populations have increased to high levels. To understand the reasons that chemicals do not provide complete control, consider the life cycle of the fungus gnat.

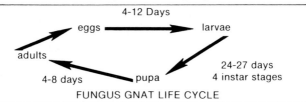

FUNGUS GNAT LIFE CYCLE

A chemical spray may be ineffective in controlling the adult fungus gnat. However, there are six other stages in the gnat's life cycle which may not be affected at all. It would take over a month of proper spraying with an insecticide that only controlled the adults, before a severe infestation of this pest was completely eradicated. Fortunately, there are sprays which will kill different insect stages as well as other methods of control, but an ounce of prevention can save a pound of trouble.

Let us discuss some of the pests that most commonly plague plants in the home:

Fungus Gnat: Although generally assumed to be harmless, the fungus gnat is one of the most common of all indoor pests. The adults are smaller than fruit flies (about 3-3½ mm), for which they are sometimes mistaken. They have black bodies with greyish-brown abdomens.

Following the cycle diagramed above, the female lays clusters of 100 to 300 eggs in the soil. At 72°F, a common home temperature, the eggs hatch in only four days. At 60°F, the eggs take 9-12 days to hatch. The emerging maggot feeds on the root hairs of young seedlings.

The larvae are easily noticed when a plant is watered. White "bugs" will be seen floating on the surface of the water. When a plant is severly infested it will lack vigor, the leaves may turn yellow, and root rots may enter through the damaged root hairs.

Prevent the problem of fungus gnats by using only sterilized potting mediums. For control of an existing problem, try using a spray at weekly intervals to control the adults and a soil insecticide to control the larvae.

White Flies: This is one of the most difficult of all indoor pests to control. Brushing the leaves of an infected plant will send these little insects fluttering. White flies lay their eggs on the undersides of leaves. The larvae feed on plant sap causing the leaves to turn yellow. If allowed to reproduce unchecked, the infested plant will soon die.

Although control of white fly is not easy, it can be accomplished. As many eggs as possible should be scraped from under the leaves by using the thumb and forefinger. In warm weather, the plant should be taken outdoors and sprayed with an appropriate chemical. The spraying should be repeated 3 to 4 times within a two week period. Undersides of leaves should be checked often for evidence of eggs, larvae, or adult white fly. If discovered, these should be mechanically removed.

Red-Spider Mite: Although these miniature pests are difficult to see with the naked eye, the damage they cause will be quite apparent. The first indication of their presence will be yellow or brown speckles on the newer foliage. If the infestation becomes great enough fine webs will be seen covering the leaves of the host plant, especially on the undersides. Infected plants slow down their growth rate and then die.

In warm weather, affected plants may be taken outdoors and sprayed with an appropriate insecticide. During the winter, strong sprays of warm water daily, will discourage the mites. Leaves may be washed occasionally with a soft cloth and soapy water to dislodge the red-spider. Plants that become severely infected may have to be discarded.

Mealy Bug: This insect resembles small clusters of cotton. They can attack all parts of a plant, but are often found in leaf axils. Mealy bugs suck a plant's sap, eventually killing the plant. Cacti and succulents seem to be a delicacy for this troublesome pest.

With patience, an infected plant can be cured. The first step is to dip a cotton swab into rubbing alcohol and touch it to the mealy bugs. Next spray the entire plant with an indoor insecticide, making sure to remain at 18 inches from the plant when spraying. The following day the plant should be washed with warm soapy water. After these steps have been taken, the treated plant should be quarantined for several weeks to make sure that the problem does not recur.

Scale: Scale insects can be the most aggravating of all indoor pests. They appear as brown blisters or as white scales. These insects often go unnoticed until the infestation has become severe. Overall yellowing or yellowing in circular spots can be a clue to this problem.

Removing the scale by hand is a tedious process, but often the most effective. A gentle washing with warm soapy water is also helpful. Spraying can be tried, but, is often ineffective, because of this insect's hard shell. In many cases it may be necessary to destroy the infected plant.

Aphids: Although this may be the most common insect pest, it is also the easiest to control. Any indoor plant spray will provide an effective control against this sucking insect. The usually greenish adult is large enough to be easily seen and may be removed by hand. Aphids reproduce rapidly and can quickly disfigure a plant if they are not checked.

Disease: Few diseases ever become a problem to the indoor gardener. Under certain conditions mildew may be a problem, in which case a systemic fungicide should provide a quick cure.

Several fungi, such as Rhizoctonia, Pythium, and Phythophthora, may cause root and stem rots, but this is usually cured by proper watering techniques. These fungi are also the causes of "damping-off" in seedlings and may be prevented through the use of sterilized soil.

Plants which are especially susceptible to various "rots" have been noted in this text. Extra care should be exercised in the watering of these particular plants, since too much water will be an invitation to problems.

Explanation of Headings

ORIGIN: Besides answering the obvious question of where a plant is found in the wild, a plant's origin can be an indication to its climatic background. Plants which are native to regions with wide temperature fluctuations may adjust to variable home conditions better than tropicals which are accustomed to constant and favorable conditions.

Knowing a plant's origin can be a key to the care it requires. For instance, a plant native of Mexico is likely to want bright light and little water. On the other hand, a plant from the tropics is apt to require opposite conditions.

FAMILY: The characteristics used to identify a plant within a family are based upon combinations of morphological (form and structural) features, especially those features of the flowers and fruit. Knowing to which family a plant belongs can reveal much information about it.

Consider the characteristics of the 'Commelinaceae' (Wandering Jew family) which includes over three dozen popular house plants: most members are terrestrial herbs with jointed stems that have alternate sheathing leaves. Their flowers are three-petaled and are often lavender in color. The fruit is usually a capsule with few seeds. Most plants in this family are trailing, excellent for hanging baskets. They desire lots of light and prefer to be kept on the dry side.

By simply knowing a plant is in this family, all these characteristics would be known.

RATING FOR HOME GROWTH: This category will give a quick indication of how well a plant adapts itself to home culture. Normally a plant will fall into one of the following groups:

    EASY — These plants adapt very well to indoor conditions. Amateurs will have their best luck with plants that receive this rating.

MODERATELY EASY — Plants which are fairly simple to grow, but one or more environmental factors which are not common indoors must be watched. For instance, a certain plant may require cool temperatures or may be extra-sensitive to over watering.

MODERATELY DIFFICULT — Plants in this category should only be grown by indoor gardeners who have had experience in growing easier plants. A novice attempting to grow such a plant would become quickly discouraged.

DIFFICULT — Even experienced gardeners have problems growing these plants. However, they are a challenge and create a feeling of accomplishment for those who succeed.

FLOWERING: Almost all green house plants, except ferns, will produce flowers. However, many of these plants will not produce flowers indoors. Lack of light and immaturity are the main reasons that house plants do not bloom. The description given for flowering includes blooms which would be produced in a natural state.

LIGHT: This is perhaps the major limiting factor for growing plants indoors. Plants described as preferring a sunny location should be given the maximum amount of light possible. These plants would be happiest near a south window, but may do well with a western exposure.

An east window would be best for plants described as needing filtered light. Light filtered through sheer curtains from a south window would also be satisfactory.

If a plant is described as tolerating low light conditions, it will probably survive in any room with some natural light source. Remember, however, that there is a difference between merely surviving and thriving. A philodendron which barely manages in a dark corner will probably burst into luxuriant growth if moved to a bright location. North windows are normally adequate for these plants.

WATERING: The watering requirements of plants will usually fall into one of the following three categories:

KEEP ON THE DRY SIDE — Plants in this group should be watered thoroughly. Then the soil should be allowed to become fairly dry before the next watering.

KEEP EVENLY MOIST, BUT NOT SOGGY — These plants should also be watered thoroughly, however, they should be watered again as the surface of the soil begins to dry. The fine roots of these plants will die without enough water and rot if they receive too much water.

KEEP CONSTANTLY WET — The plants which fall into this classification are either bog plants or aquatic varieties. Generally speaking, they cannot be over watered.

SOIL: The recommendations given are for those enthusiasts who blend their own potting mixtures. There are many commercial mixes on the market which are usually adequate for any need that might arise. Use the given soil mixtures as a guide to adjust a commercial mix. For instance, if a plant requires a highly organic soil, add leaf mold to your potting soil. If the plant requires a well-drained soil, add sand, perlite, or vermiculite to your soil.

PRUNING: Since few plants are naturally small or compact, pruning and shaping are necessary to produce bushy and attractive plants. Many new gardeners cannot bring themselves to pinch out the growing tips of their plant, but this is a horticulturally sound practice.

The growing tips of plants produce a hormone called auxin which inhibits the development of axillary buds. Because of this, many plants will grow to be tall and slender with few leaves. However, if the terminal bud is removed (pinched off), new growth will usually begin in two axillary buds just below where the cut was made. After the new branches have begun to grow, they may also be pinched back. This repeated pruning will help to maintain a more attractive and compact plant.

Information At A Glance

For quick reference, the following symbols may be found in the upper right hand corner of the appropriate plant pictures. Although the symbols are not complete guides, they will provide fast clues to plant characteristics.

HANGING BASKETS — Plants which bear this symbol are either trailing or vining and ideally suited for hanging baskets.

CACTUS OR SUCCULENT — These plants are native to arid regions and must be kept on the dry side. This group is especially sensitive to overwatering.

FLOWERS OR COLORFUL FOLIAGE — While most plants flower, this symbol represents those which are grown especially for their flowers. It may also indicate a plant not known for its bloom, but for its highly colorful foliage.

BEAUTIFUL FOLIAGE PLANTS — Mainly plants with outstanding green foliage. This group includes most of the oldtime favorites.

TERRARIUM PLANTS — Plants which are commonly used in terrariums, either because of compact size or high humidity requirements.

Hanging Baskets

The current popularity of hanging baskets has enabled plant lovers to utilize yet another dimension for room decor. Aside from its charm, the use of a suspended container creates an eye-level garden which permits the best display of trailing plants and vines. A vining philodendron in a macrame rope hanger is more appealing than it could ever be sitting on a windowsill.

There is a multitude of plants, having leaves of various shapes and sizes, for use in either sunny or shady locations. Remember, however, that no plant will survive for any length of time in a room without windows, unless it is provided with 14 to 16 hours of artificial light daily. For this reason, it is important to choose a location which satisfies the light requirements of your particular plant.

Elegant, full grown baskets can be obtained from your local garden center at very reasonable prices. Empty baskets are also available for the person who wants to start his own. A general rule of thumb would be to use one 2¼" pot-size plant for every 2" of basket diameter. For example, 3 plants of this size should be used in a 6" diameter planter; 4 plants in an eight inch diameter basket, and so forth.

The material that the planter is made from is insignificant, however, it is important that the pot has a drainage hole. Many beautiful ceramic planters should not be used because they are not equipped with a drain hole. Plastic planters with attached saucers seem to be best for indoor use. Wire baskets, lined with moss, are extremely popular, but because of watering difficulty, are better used outdoors.

Utilization of hanging containers is increasing both indoors and outdoors. They save space, and keep plants out of the reach of pets and small children.

ASPARAGUS FERN
(Asparagus sprengeri)

ORIGIN: West Africa
FAMILY: Liliaceae

**RATING FOR HOME
GROWTH:** Easy

FLOWERING: Very small, white, fragrant flowers followed by red berries.
LIGHT: Filtered sun.
WATERING: Allow to slightly dry between waterings.
SOIL: Equal parts loam, sand, and peat moss.
PRUNING: None.

For years the asparagus fern has been treated as an annual and used as a compliment to geranium tubs. Lately more people have come to respect the plant for its own merits. The cascading branches are shown off nicely in a hanging basket. Cut branches of the needlelike foliage are a welcome addition to floral arrangements.

Though easy to care for, low light conditions can cause the needles to drop. Propagate the asparagus fern by seed or by division of large clumps.

CANDLE PLANT
(Plectranthus coleoides 'Marginatus')

ORIGIN: S. India
FAMILY: Labiatae

RATING FOR HOME GROWTH: Moderately difficult

FLOWERING: Small white with purple flowers in erect racemes.
LIGHT: Filtered sun.
WATERING: Never let soil become soggy, but equally important not to let it dry out.
SOIL: Equal parts loam, peat, and perlite.
PRUNING: Pinch to encourage branching.

The square stems and very aromatic foliage of the candle plant are typical of members of the mint family. Although more bushy than vining, the dark green leaves with scalloped creamy-white margins make this an especially attractive plant for hanging baskets.

The candle plant is not as easy to grow as its cousin, the Swedish ivy. Overwatering is probably the major problem in its culture, however a well drained soil should help to compensate. The candle plant can easily be propagated by stem-tip cuttings.

CREEPING IMPATIENS
(Impatiens repens)

ORIGIN: Ceylon
FAMILY: Balsaminaceae

RATING FOR HOME GROWTH: Moderately easy

FLOWERING: Hooded, yellow-gold flowers.
LIGHT: Filtered light.
WATERING: Allow to slightly dry between waterings.
SOIL: Equal parts loam, sand, peat moss, and leaf mold.
PRUNING: Pinch to encourage branching.

Fleshy red branches and kidney-shaped leaves, make this species of impatiens a very unusual plant. Virtually an unknown several years ago, the creeping impatiens is gaining in popularity. Unfortunately, it is still difficult to locate and may require some searching before you find a nursery or greenhouse that carries it.

The flowers on this plant are completely unexpected. They are larger and shaped differently than the garden variety of impatiens. As with all impatiens, red spider mites may become a problem. Frequent overhead sprayings with lukewarm water will discourage the mites. Propagate your creeping impatiens by stem-tip cuttings.

ENGLISH BABY TEARS
(Pilea depressa)

ORIGIN: Puerto Rico
FAMILY: Urticaceae

RATING FOR HOME GROWTH: Easy

FLOWERING: Insignificant, greenish flowers in axillary clusters.
LIGHT: Filtered light.
WATERING: Keep evenly moist, but not soggy.
SOIL: Equal parts loam, sand, and peat moss.
PRUNING: Not needed.

The tiny ¼", glossy, light green leaves of this species of pilea made it extremely popular as a ground cover in terrariums and dish gardens. However its rapid growth makes it more suitable as a basket subject. Place four plants in a 6" basket for an immediate effect.

Insects seldom plague the English baby tears. Proper light and water will almost guarantee a plant of which to be proud. Like other pilea species it can be easily propagated by stem-tip cuttings.

ENGLISH IVY
(Hedera helix)

ORIGIN: Asia, Europe, N. Africa
FAMILY: Araliaceae

RATING FOR HOME GROWTH: Moderately easy

FLOWERING: Insignificant.
LIGHT: Sunny to part sun.
WATERING: Saturate soil and allow to dry before next watering.
SOIL: Equal parts loam, sand, and peat moss.
PRUNING: Pinch back to encourage branching.

More people have probably tried and failed in growing ivies than any other plant. One of the main reasons for this is high home temperatures. Ivies prefer winter temperatures under 70°F. The plant will also need frequent overhead sprayings to discourage red spider mites which are often a problem.

Another important factor is good lighting. This is especially true for the variegated varieties. Under low light conditions, your ivy will drop its leaves one by one. In spite of some difficulty in care, English ivy is definitely worth growing. It does tolerate draft near doors and air conditioning. Propagate your ivy by stem-tip cuttings.

FLAME VIOLET
(Episcia cupreata)

ORIGIN: Colombia
FAMILY: Gesneriaceae

RATING FOR HOME GROWTH: Moderately easy

FLOWERING: Brilliant shades of orange-red, depending on variety; also a yellow variety 'Tropical Topaz'.
LIGHT: Filtered light.
WATERING: Keep evenly moist, but not soggy.
SOIL: Should be rich in humus, with equal parts loam, sand, peat moss and leaf mold.
PRUNING: None.

Anyone who has grown african violets must eventually try to grow episcias. Their handsome quilted and velvety foliage makes them attractive even when not in bloom.

There are several basic steps which must be followed for successful episcia culture. First, remember to use lukewarm water. Cold water will spot the leaves as it does to the african violet. Also, keep in mind that these plants are extremely cold sensitive and begin suffering below 65° F. Misting in the winter months will help increase the humidity which your flame violet will need to thrive.

Propagation can be accomplished by rooting the strawberry-like offsets which these plants produce.

GERMAN IVY

(Senecio mikanioides)

ORIGIN: South Africa
FAMILY: Compositae

**RATING FOR HOME
GROWTH:** Easy

FLOWERING: Yellow-disk flowers, uncommon in the home.
LIGHT: Filtered sun.
WATERING: Keep evenly moist, but not soggy.
SOIL: Equal parts loam, sand, and peat moss.
PRUNING: Pinch tips to encourage branching.

German ivy makes a good windowsill plant or hanging basket plant near a window, since it prefers cooler temperatures and bright light. Ideal conditions are night temperatures of 60°-75°F and daytime temperatures of 65°-75°F.

The thin, bright-green, ivylike leaves make this plant an attractive basket candidate, but remember that even under ideal conditions it is not a rapid grower. If sufficient light is available, the major problem in growing German ivy is likely to be overwatering. Soggy soil for any extended period of time is sure to lead to the plant's demise. New plants can be easily produced by stem-tip cuttings.

GIANT WHITE INCH PLANT
(Tradescantia albiflora 'Albo-vittata')

ORIGIN: Central America
FAMILY: Commelinaceae

**RATING FOR HOME
GROWTH:** Easy

FLOWERING: Three-petaled white flowers.
LIGHT: Filtered light.
WATERING: Let soil partially dry between waterings.
SOIL: Equal parts loam, sand, and peat moss.
PRUNING: Pinch heavily to encourage branching.

The common name of inch plants comes from their growth rate—they rapidly "inch" along. The 3" to 4" leaves are large compared to other members of the family.

Of all the inch plants, this one probably has the greatest tendency to become straggly. If this happens simply place six stem-tip cuttings to an eight inch basket. This plant easily roots at every node.

GOLDEN POTHOS
(Scindapsus aureus)

ORIGIN; Solomon Islands
FAMILY: Araceae

RATING FOR HOME GROWTH: Easy

FLOWERING: Spadix within a boat-shaped spathe.
LIGHT: Filtered light.
WATERING: Allow to nearly dry between waterings.
SOIL: Equal parts loam, sand, peat moss, and leaf mold.
PRUNING: Pinch to encourage branching.

Most plant enthusiasts have had a pothos that trailed half way around a room at some time in their growing experience. For years, it has been one of the more popular houseplants since it thrives in high temperatures, it is especially suited to indoor culture.

Except for its color, the pothos so closely resembles a philodendron, that it is often called "variegated philodendron". The care of the two plants is similar except for the light requirements. More light tends to improve the variegation of the golden pothos. Propagation may be accomplished by stem-tip cuttings.

GOLDEN POTHOS

GOLDFISH PLANT
(Hypocyrta wettsteinii)

ORIGIN: Tropical America
FAMILY: Gesneriaceae

RATING FOR HOME GROWTH: Moderately difficult

FLOWERING: Orange-yellow, pouch-shaped flowers.
LIGHT: Filtered light.
WATERING: Keep evenly moist, but not soggy.
SOIL: Equal parts loam, sand, peat moss and leaf mold.
PRUNING: Occasional pinching to encourage branching.

The goldfish plant is a beautiful subject for hanging baskets, but somewhat difficult to grow because of its requirements for warmth and high humidity. When in bloom, the bright yellow flowers mimic a school of plump little goldfish. Aside from the flowers, the glossy green leaves of the goldfish plant are also an attraction.

Although this plant blooms mainly in the summer and fall it will be in almost constant bloom under good conditions. Bright light is an important fact in blossoming. Fourteen to sixteen hours a day of artificial lighting will substitute for natural light.

Monthly fertilizing during active growing periods should be performed. The goldfish plant can be propagated from stem cuttings at any time of the year.

GRAPE IVY
(Cissus rhombifolia)

ORIGIN: West Indies
FAMILY: Vitaceae

RATING FOR HOME GROWTH: Easy

FLOWERING: Small four-petaled flowers.
LIGHT: Filtered light.
WATERING: Keep evenly moist, but not soggy.
SOIL: Equal parts loam, sand, and peat moss.
PRUNING: Pinch to shape.

Grape ivy with its brown, hairy branches and coiling tendrils is another oldtime favorite houseplant. Besides the branches, the new leaf buds are also covered with a soft brown fuzz. This is one of the best ramblers for a living room or office and it seems to do well under air conditioning.

Grape ivy is actually a member of the grape family and at one time was even classified in the same genus as edible grapes. It is relatively easy to care for, with red spider mites sometimes being a problem. Frequent overhead sprayings with water will help to eliminate the red spider. New plants may be started from stem-tip cuttings.

HEARTLEAF PHILODENDRON
(Philodendron oxycardium)

ORIGIN: Central America
FAMILY: Araceae

RATING FOR HOME GROWTH: Easy

FLOWERING: Not significant.
LIGHT: Tolerates low light.
WATERING: Keep evenly moist, but not soggy.
SOIL: Equal parts loam, sand, and peat moss.
PRUNING: Pinch to control shape.

Almost everyone who grows indoor plants tries to grow a philodendron at sometime or another. For years this has been the most popular and widely grown of all houseplants, and justly so. The philly will survive in places where most other plants will not. It silently ignores almost any abuse given to it.

Although it will grow under poor conditions, the plant will not be at its best. The leaves of the philodendron will be noticeably smaller under low light conditions and the leaves will lose some of their luster.

Besides making an excellent basket planter, the philodendron is often grown on poles and used as a floor plant. Propagate it by stem-tip cuttings.

KANGAROO IVY
(Cissus antarctica)

ORIGIN: New South Wales
FAMILY: Vitaceae

RATING FOR HOME GROWTH: Easy

FLOWERING: Insignificant.
LIGHT: Filtered sun.
WATERING: Allow to slightly dry between waterings.
SOIL: Equal parts loam, sand, and peat moss.
PRUNING: None.

Kangaroo ivy is not grown as often as its cousin grape ivy, but it too is of value. Its shining green leaves, with saw-toothed edges may grow to six inches. This vigorous vine tolerates low humidity and lower temperatures than many houseplants. However if winter home temperatures go much over 72° F, there may be a tendency for the leaves to turn brown and fall off.

This is definitely a plant for larger hanging baskets. Plant four or five plants to an eight or ten inch basket for a bushier effect. Kangaroo ivy is propagated from stem-tip cuttings.

LIPSTICK VINE
(Aeschynanthus pulcher)

ORIGIN: Java
FAMILY: Gesneriaceae

RATING FOR HOME GROWTH: Difficult

FLOWERING: Scarlet, tubular flowers with yellow throats
LIGHT: Filtered light.
WATERING: Keep evenly moist, but not soggy.
SOIL: Equal parts loam, sand, peat moss, and leaf mold.
PRUNING: None.

Unfortunately, the highly humid conditions in which lipstick vines thrive, are not easily produced in the home. For good growth, they require humidities in the range of 50 to 70 per cent. Still, for the person who likes challenges, the lipstick vine is certainly worth trying.

At the end of a stem, a brown calyx forms with a scarlet bud inside. Before the bud opens it resembles lipstick inside a tube, thus the common name of this plant. Propagate lipstick vines from stem-tip cuttings.

PIGGYBACK PLANT
(*Tolmiea menziesii*)

ORIGIN: N. American West Coast
FAMILY: Saxifragaceae

RATING FOR HOME GROWTH: Easy

FLOWERING: Small, green flowers on a thin raceme.
LIGHT: Filtered light.
WATERING: Keep evenly moist, but not soggy.
SOIL: Equal parts loam, sand, and peat moss.
PRUNING: None.

Piggyback is an oldtime favorite houseplant. Adults as well as children are intrigued by the new plantlets that "ride" on the "backs" of mature leaves.

In sheltered areas outdoors this plant may be winter hardy. If you attempt to grow the piggyback outdoors, plant it in a moist, shady location. Although the blossom are not particularly attractive, the plant will probably bloom if grown outdoors. Propagate the piggyback plant by rooting the mature leaves with small plantlets in moist vermiculite.

PURPLE HEART
(Setcreasea purpurea)

ORIGIN: Mexico
FAMILY: Commelinaceae

RATING FOR HOME GROWTH: Easy

FLOWERING: Three-petaled, lilac colored flowers.
LIGHT: Sun to part sun.
WATERING: Allow to partially dry between waterings.
SOIL: Equal parts loam, sand, and peat moss.
PRUNING: Pinch to encourage branching

Being one of the few house plants with purple foliage draws immediate attention to the purple heart. Besides its leafy attraction, there is the welcome addition of the deep-lilac colored flowers.

This plant is often used as a ground cover in Florida and southern California, so it is a sun lover. Though it will tolerate low light conditions, a sunny exposure is necessary to bring out the vivid purple coloring in the leaves. Purple heart is grown to its best advantage in a hanging basket where its trailing stems can cascade over the sides. It can be easily propagated by stem-tip cuttings.

PURPLE PASSION VINE
(Gynura sarmentosa)

ORIGIN: Southeast Asia
FAMILY: Compositae

RATING FOR HOME GROWTH: Easy

FLOWERING: Orange-yellow, dandelion-like flowers.
LIGHT: Sunny.
WATERING: Keep evenly moist, but not soggy.
SOIL: Equal parts loam, sand, and peat moss.
PRUNING: Pinch to encourage branching.

The purple hairs covering the leaves of the purple passion give it a velvety appearance which makes it one of the fastest selling plants on the market today. However, it does have one minor disadvantage. This plant produces a flower bud which looks like it should produce a beautiful flower. Instead you are disappointed by some sickly looking orange disk type flowers which smell like someone's stinky stockings. Because of this, it is advisable to keep the buds pinched off.

A sunny location is necessary for the purple passion to show its best color. It quickly fades under low light intensities. Propagation can be accomplished by means of stem-tip cuttings.

PURPLE PASSION VINE

RED IVY
(Hemigraphis colorata)

ORIGIN: Java
FAMILY: Acanthaceae

RATING FOR HOME
GROWTH: Easy

FLOWERING: Small white flowers.
LIGHT: Tolerates low light conditions, but color is more vivid in sunnier locations.
WATERING: Keep evenly moist, not soggy.
SOIL: Two parts humus to one part loam and sand.
PRUNING: Pinch back to encourage branching.

Red ivy is a plant which deserves more popularity. The unusual leaf color and occasional flowers make an interesting basket. The leaves have a silverish cast to them under lower light conditions and a reddish-purple color in semi-sun. This plant prefers the higher humidities, but seems to do well in the average home.

There is also a variety called 'exotica' with wine-red puckered leaves that is worth mentioning. Commonly known as "waffle plant", it has smaller leaves and is more bushy than the specie. Either plant may easily be propagated by stem-tip cuttings.

SATIN PELLIONIA
(Pellionia daveauana)

ORIGIN: Vietnam
FAMILY: Urticaceae

**RATING FOR HOME
GROWTH:** Easy.

FLOWERING: Small green flowers.
LIGHT: Filtered light.
WATERING: Keep evenly moist, but not soggy.
SOIL: Equal parts loam, sand, and peat moss.
PRUNING: Pinch to shape.

Satin pellionia is fairly uncommon houseplant also known as watermelon begonia. It is surprising that this plant is not grown more, since it adapts very well to indoor conditions. Pellionia thrive in the warm climate of today's homes.

Besides use in hanging baskets, pellionia can also be used as a ground cover in larger terrariums. There is another species, P. pulchra, with the same growing habits, but more colorful leaves. Either species may be propagated by stem-tip cuttings.

SPIDER PLANT
(Chlorophytum comosum 'Vittatum')

ORIGIN: South Africa
FAMILY: Liliaceae

RATING FOR HOME GROWTH: Easy

FLOWERING: Small white flowers.
LIGHT: Filtered sun.
WATERING: Allow to partially dry between waterings.
SOIL: Equal parts loam, sand, and peat moss.
PRUNING: None.

The spider plant sends out long, slender racemes of small white flowers which are followed by new plantlets ("spiders"). As these new plants become larger, they cause the stems to bend over, creating a dramatic effect in a hanging basket.

New plants may be produced by removing the aerial plantlets and potting them. Besides the variegated spider plant there is also a green form which is faster growing. Both types are easy to grow and seem to thrive on neglect. For some unexplainable reason the leaf tips sometimes turn brown. If this happens simply snip off the brown portion.

STRAWBERRY BEGONIA
(Saxifraga sarmentosa)

ORIGIN: China
FAMILY: Saxifragaceae

**RATING FOR HOME
GROWTH:** Easy

FLOWERING: White flowers on tall, thin stalks.
LIGHT: Prefers sunny location.
WATERING: Allow to partially dry between waterings.
SOIL: Equal parts loam, sand, and peat moss.
PRUNING: None.

Although it is neither a strawberry nor a begonia, this plant spreads by strawberry-like runners which bear young plantlets. It also gets its name from the white veins on its leaves which are characteristic of some begonias. The strawberry begonia is probably more popular as a terrarium plant than as a basket plant, but it performs well in either capacity.

There is also a variety of this plant which is known as 'Magic Carpet'. This variety is brightly colored, but very difficult to grow. The strawberry begonia may be propagated by removing the young plantlets and rooting them.

STRING OF HEARTS
(Ceropegia woodii)

ORIGIN: Natal
FAMILY: Asclepiadaceae

**RATING FOR HOME
GROWTH:** Easy

FLOWERING: Unusual, purple tubular flowers.
LIGHT: Filtered sun.
WATERING: Keep on the dry side.
SOIL: Equal parts loam, sand, peat moss, and leaf mold.
PRUNING: Pinch to encourage branching.

String of hearts forms a chain of small, grey, heart-shaped leaves that are speckled with green. Small tubers form at the internodes on the vine, which is why the plant is also known as rosary vine.

Because of its small size, the string of hearts should be grown in a small basket or on a small trellis. The plant is actually more unusual than attractive, and is still somewhat difficult to locate. If your local nursery does not carry this plant it can sometimes be mail ordered from greenhouses advertising in horticultural magazines. Cuttings can be rooted or the plant may be propagated from the tubers which it forms.

STRING OF PEARLS
(Senecio herreianus)

ORIGIN: S.W. Africa
FAMILY: Compositae

**RATING FOR HOME
GROWTH:** Moderately easy

FLOWERING: Light yellow, daisy-like flowers.
LIGHT: Sunny.
WATERING: Keep on dry side.
SOIL: Equal parts loam, sand, and peat moss.
PRUNING: None.

One of the most unusual of all succulents, the berry-like, green leaves of this plant actually resemble a string of beads. This is an excellent plant for a six inch basket and for the person who wants something unusual. At the present time, the demand for this plant exceeds the supply so it is slightly higher priced than most other succulents.

Don't forget that the string of pearls is a succulent and will not tolerate wet soils. It also needs a sunny exposure. The string of pearls can be propagated from cuttings.

STRIPED INCH PLANT
(Callisia elegans)

ORIGIN: Mexico
FAMILY: Commelinaceae

RATING FOR HOME GROWTH: Easy

FLOWERING: Three-petaled white flowers.
LIGHT: Filtered light.
WATERING: Keep evenly moist, but not soggy.
SOIL: Equal parts loam, sand and peat moss.
PRUNING: Pinch to encourage branching.

It is hard to imagine why so little is ever written about the striped inch plant. It is easy to grow and has attractive olive green leaves lined with white stripes and purple undersides. The small white flowers are an added bonus to the foliage.

This plant may not always be available from your local nursery, but it is worth shopping around for. An excellent item for hanging baskets, its popularity may soon increase. Once you have found a plant you can propagate it as other members of the family, by stem-tip cuttings.

SWEDISH IVY
(Plectranthus australis)

ORIGIN: Australia
FAMILY: Labiatae

RATING FOR HOME GROWTH: Easy

FLOWERING: Small white flowers in spikes.
LIGHT: Filtered sun.
WATERING: Keep evenly moist, but not soggy.
SOIL: Equal parts loam, sand, and peat moss.
PRUNING: Pinch growing tips to encourage dense branching.

Although it is a native of Australia, this plant gets its common name from the fact that is was first widely used as a house plant in Sweden. With the current popularity of hanging baskets, the waxy, green, scalloped leaves of the Swedish ivy are becoming a more frequent sight in American homes.

Besides the solid green form, there is also a variegated variety which is being widely grown. This plant requires little care and grows quite fast under good conditions. New plants can be very easily produced by stem-tip cuttings.

SWEETHEART IVY
(Hedera helix 'Scutifolia')

ORIGIN: Variety of H. helix
FAMILY: Araliaceae

RATING FOR HOME GROWTH: Moderately easy

FLOWERING: Insignificant.
LIGHT: Sunny to part sun.
WATERING: Saturate soil and allow to dry before next watering.
SOIL: Equal parts loam, sand, and peat moss.
PRUNING: Pinch back to encourage branching.

Sweetheart ivy, with its small heart-shaped leaves, has become a popular gift for Valentine's Day. This variety has basically this same cultural requirements as the specie. It is slower growing than English ivy and should be provided with the maximum amount of available light to grow at its best.

Propagate this ivy, as others, by stem-tip cuttings.

SWEETHEART IVY

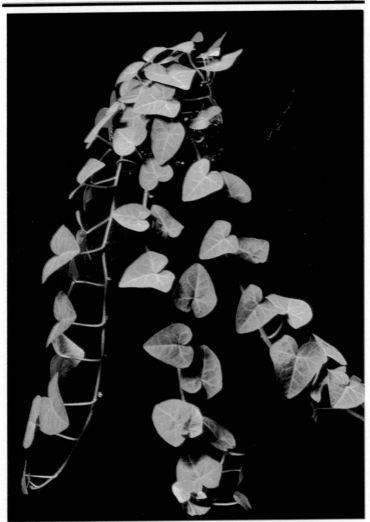

TAHITIAN BRIDAL VEIL
(Tradescantia multiflora)

ORIGIN: Tropical America
FAMILY: Commelinaceae

RATING FOR HOME GROWTH: Easy

FLOWERING: Small white flowers.
LIGHT: Sunny.
WATERING: Keep on the dry side.
SOIL: Equal parts loam, sand, and peat moss.
PRUNING: Cut back for shaping.

Bridal veil is certainly an appropriate name for this plant. Once it has become established, the cascading branches are literally covered with tiny white blossoms calling to mind a bride's veil. The leaves are small, about one inch, and are dark green with purple undersides.

Tahitian bridal veil is a rampant grower. Three or four small plants will fill out an eight inch basket in no time at all. When pruning the plant, stick the cuttings back into the soil and they will root without any extra care.

TEDDY-BEAR VINE
(Cyanotis kewensis)

ORIGIN: India
FAMILY: Commelinaceae

RATING FOR HOME GROWTH: Easy

FLOWERING: Small purple flowers.
LIGHT: Sunny.
WATERING: Keep on dry side.
SOIL: Equal parts loam, sand, and peat moss.
PRUNING: Little needed; pinch only to encourage branching.

The teddy-bear vine gets its name from the velvety brown hair covering its stems and leaves. Since it is very slow growing it is best to keep it in a hanging basket that is six inches or less.

This plant prefers drier conditions and a sunnier location than other members of the family. Insects are rarely a problem and the vine is relatively carefree. An unfortunate fact that the plant is so slow growing that few commercial growers are willing to trouble themselves with it. If the plant cannot be found at your local nursery, find a friend who is willing to part with a piece. The teddy-bear vine propagates easily from stem-tip cuttings.

VINING PEPEROMIA
(Peperomia scandens)

ORIGIN: Peru
FAMILY: Piperaceae

RATING FOR HOME GROWTH: Easy

FLOWERING: Insignificant white flowers on thin spikes.
LIGHT: Filtered light.
WATERING: Keep on dry side.
SOIL: Equal parts loam, sand, and peat moss.
PRUNING: Pinch to keep from getting leggy.

The name, "peperomia", means pepper-like and all peperomias are members of the black pepper family. The waxy, heart-shaped leaves of the vining peperomia make it an attractive candidate for hanging baskets.

All peperomias are warmth-loving and easy to grow indoors. Overwatering can be a serious problem with these plants. Under wet conditions, they are extremely susceptible to the phytophthora fungus which causes a rotting of stems near the base of the plant. Many peperomia may be started from single leaves, but the vining peperomia is more easily propagated by stem-tip cuttings.

WANDERING JEW
(Zebrina pendula)

ORIGIN: Mexico
FAMILY: Commelinaceae

RATING FOR HOME GROWTH: Easy

FLOWERING: Three-petaled, rosy-purple flowers in spring and summer.
LIGHT: Sun to part sun.
WATERING: Let soil partially dry between waterings.
SOIL: Equal parts loam, sand, and peat moss.
PRUNING: Pinch to encourage branching.

The wandering jew will exist under poor growing conditions, but will also look like it has been neglected. A sunny location is desirable for best leaf color and the cheery little flowers it produces.

The wandering jew family has probably been the family that has most benefitted from the recent popularity of hanging baskets. There are a number of members with similar characteristics such as attractive three-petaled flowers and colorful or interesting foliage. This plant as well as others in the family can easily be propagated by stem-tip cuttings.

WAX IVY

(Senecio macroglossus variegatus)

ORIGIN: Kenya
FAMILY: Compositae

RATING FOR HOME GROWTH: Easy

FLOWERING: White daisy-like flowers with yellow centers.
LIGHT: Filtered sun.
WATERING: Keep on dry side.
SOIL: Equal parts loam, sand, and peat moss.
PRUNING: Pinch to encourage branching.

Here's a real plant that actually looks more like an artificial. Its sharp colors and waxy appearance give it a plastic look. Whether or not this is an advantage becomes academic as this plant increases in popularity.

Though not a true ivy (Hedera), this vine is a very prolific grower with a twining habit. Overwatering is likely to be a problem with some people. This plant is a succulent and likes to dry between waterings. The wax ivy also likes warmer temperatures and a little more light than its cousin, the German ivy. Propagate by stem-tip cuttings.

WAX PLANT
(Hoya carnosa variegata)

ORIGIN: Australia, S. China   **RATING FOR HOME**
FAMILY: Asclepiadaceae   **GROWTH:** Easy

FLOWERING: Clusters of pinkish-white fragrant flowers.
LIGHT: Filtered sun.
WATERING: Keep on the dry side, especially in winter.
SOIL: Equal parts loam, sand, peat moss, and leaf mold.
PRUNING: A little pinching to encourage branching.

The wax plant derives its name from both its waxy leaves and its beautiful wax-like clusters of flowers. Each flower in the cluster has a star-shaped crown in its center and a splendid fragrance.

To bring a wax plant into bloom requires some patience. It is important not to disturb the plant when it is in bud, since even a change in light direction may cause the wax plant to drop its buds. Remember never to cut off old flowers, since new flowers are produced on the same spurs year after year.

Variegated forms of this plant seem to be easier to grow, but do not flower as frequently as the green form. In any case the most important factor to watch is watering. Overwatering can quickly kill this plant.

Notes

Ferns and Foliage Plants

FERNS: Most ferns are not difficult to raise, but the low humidity of many homes in the winter can create problems. Daily misting with an atomizer (using distilled water to prevent salt build-up) may help. A dry atmosphere may also encourage the presence of insects such as mealybug and scale. Mechanical removal may be the only cure for this problem, since many ferns are extremely sensitive to chemical sprays.

The easiest ways to propagate ferns are by division, rooting of runners, or removal of suckers, depending upon the type of fern being reproduced. Most ferns may also be propagated from spores. Unfortunately, this is a long and tedious process.

Spores must be sown on moist soil. Here, they germinate into a flat leaf-like organ which produces male and female parts on its underside. These unite through a drop of water and the fern plant as we know it is born. Although the production of ferns from spores is reliable, it should be left to home horticulturists with an abundance of patience.

Apart from true ferns, there is a group of fern-like plants which are not actually ferns. This includes the asparagus fern, the peacock ferns, and even the "air-fern" (which incidentally, is not even a plant, but the dyed skeletal remains of a moss animal of the genus Bugula which lives in the sea).

FOLIAGE PLANTS: Like the ferns, the foliage plants described are grown mainly for their greenery. All these plants bloom, but their flowering indoors is either rare or insignificant. Their uses are many: indoor trees, dish gardens and terrariums.

Although experienced indoor gardeners will want to grow more challenging plants, the green adapt very well to the home environment and are irreplaceable as decorating pieces. A violet may thrive on a windowsill, but nothing can brighten up a dim corner like a heartleaf philodendron. The green foliage plants are here to stay.

BABY'S TEARS
(Helxine soleirolii)

ORIGIN: Corsica, Sardinia
FAMILY: Urticaceae

**RATING FOR HOME
GROWTH:** Moderately easy

FLOWERING: Minute greenish-white flowers.
LIGHT: Filtered light.
WATERING: Keep evenly moist, but not soggy.
SOIL: Equal parts loam, sand, peat moss, and leaf mold.
PRUNING: None.

Baby's tears is probably the most sought after plant for terrarium use. The tiny orbicular leaves of about ¼" form dense mats of ground cover. The plant spreads very rapidly once it has been established, but requires high humidity. If grown in a pot, it is best to locate it on a windowsill above the sink and mist it daily.

In California, this plant is becoming popular as a filler in outdoor hanging baskets. There is also a gold-leaved variety which is being used more. Baby's tears is easily propagated by allowing it to ramble across soil in a propagating pot and rooting itself.

BIRDSNEST FERN
(Asplenium nidus)

ORGIN: Asia
FAMILY: Filices

RATING FOR HOME GROWTH: Moderately easy

FLOWERING: None.
LIGHT: Filtered light.
WATERING: Keep evenly moist, but not soggy.
SOIL: Equal parts loam, sand, peat moss, and leaf mold.
PRUNING: None.

The foliage of the birdsnest fern is definitely not characteristic of most ferns. The simple, glossy green fronds which rise in rosettes, are contrasted by black midribs and wavy leaf margins. A striking accent plant, a mature birdsnest fern is one of the most beautiful of all foliage plants.

Although it is fairly easy to grow, cold drafts or underwatering will cause the new fronds of this fern to be deformed. Leaf cleaners may also destroy the fronds, so they should not be used.

Scale insects can also be a problem with the birdsnest fern. The only sure and safe method of removing them is by patiently rubbing them off with a cotton swab dipped in rubbing alcohol.

Propagation is a difficult process from spores or by removal of small plantlets which may appear around the base of older plants.

BOSTON FERN
(Nephrolepis exaltata bostoniensis)

ORIGIN: Cultivar of
N. exaltata,
discovered in Boston
FAMILY: Filices

**RATING FOR HOME
GROWTH:** Moderately easy

FLOWERING: None.
LIGHT: Filtered sun.
WATERING: Keep evenly moist, but not soggy.
SOIL: Equal parts loam, sand, and peat moss.
PRUNING: None.

This is the plant that most people think of when the word "fern" is mentioned. Once considered to be old-fashioned, ferns are enjoying an amazing ressurgence in popularity. The Boston variety, first found in Boston in the 1890's, has produced around 100 varieties with different leaflet structures and growing habits.

Many people have the mistaken idea that ferns grow in dark places. On the contrary, most ferns including the Boston fern need a bright light. Fronds may turn brown in winter, because of low humidity. If this happens, frequent misting with distilled water may help.

Propagate your Boston fern by pinning runners to soil and allowing new plants to develop.

BUDDHIST PINE
(Podocarpus macrophyllus)

ORIGIN: China, Japan
FAMILY: Podocarpaceae

RATING FOR HOME GROWTH: Easy

FLOWERING: Male flowers are catkin-like, female flowers are small and green.
LIGHT: Sunny.
WATERING: Keep evenly moist, but not soggy.
SOIL: Equal parts loam, sand, and peat moss.
PRUNING: Prune only to shape.

The buddhist pine is one of those plants that deserves more popularity. Although they grow to be large trees in their native habitat, they are extremely slow growing under indoor culture. In fact, very small plants are often planted in terrariums. Old specimen plants indoors seldom reach more than six to eight feet.

Though they prefer sun by nature, the buddhist pine will tolerate low light conditions. This plant does appreciate good air circulation and a summer spent outdoors will help strengthen it for the winter months inside. Propagate it from seeds or cuttings which have not quite hardened.

BUTTON FERN
(Pellaea rotundifolia)

ORIGIN: New Zealand
FAMILY: Filices

RATING FOR HOME
GROWTH: Moderately easy

FLOWERING: None
LIGHT: Filtered light
WATERING: Keep evenly moist, but not soggy
SOIL: Equal parts loam, sand, and peat moss
PRUNING: None

One of the pleasant results of the recent interest in ferns has been the increased availability of this little gem. The fronds of the button fern are made up of small, leathery, dark-green, button-like leaflets which become more oblong as the plant gets older. This unusual foliage makes the button fern a much sought after plant.

Because of its small size, this miniature fern is an excellent subject for terrarium use. The higher humidity of the terrarium provides an ideal condition for the button fern.

Propagation can be accomplished by the sowing of spores or by the division of older plants.

CHINESE EVERGREEN
(Aglaonema commutatum elegans)

ORIGIN: Molucca Islands
FAMILY: Araceae

RATING FOR HOME GROWTH: Easy

FLOWERING: Spathe and spadix.
LIGHT: Tolerates low light conditions.
WATERING: Keep evenly moist, but not soggy.
SOIL: Equal parts loam, sand, and peat moss.
PRUNING: None.

Perhaps the most attractive feature about the Chinese evergreen is that it seems to thrive on neglect. It tolerates dark conditions, so it is a perfect plant to set on that coffee table away from the window. Because of its small size, it is an excellent plant choice for dish gardens.

The Chinese evergreen does not seem to be fussy over its water requirements. Allowing it to become dry before watering appears to be just fine with this plant. On the other hand, if you are interested in hydroponics, this is a good plant because it grows just fine in plain water.

The flowers of the Chinese evergreen are not especially pretty, but they are followed by bright red berries if pollinated.

Fertilizing is not important to this plant. Use a 5-10-5 three times per year and that should be sufficient.

COFFEE PLANT
(Coffea arabica)

ORIGIN: Tropical Africa
FAMILY: Rubiaceae

**RATING FOR HOME
GROWTH:** Moderately difficult

FLOWERING: Fragrant white flowers.
LIGHT: Filtered light.
WATERING: Keep evenly moist, but not soggy.
SOIL: Equal parts loam, sand, and peat moss.
PRUNING: Pinch to shape.

There seems to be a certain mystery in growing tropical food plants such as avocadoes, citrus, and pineapple indoors. Growing your own coffee plant seems to hold equally as much intrigue. If enough light and humidity can be supplied, indoor growth is not really much of a problem.

The shiny, dark-green foliage of the coffee is handsome in its own right. However the main attraction are the bright-red, cherry-like berries which contain the coffee beans on mature plants. These beans take several months to ripen and may be dried and actually used for coffee or sown immediately to produce new plants.

DRAGON PALM
(Dracaena marginata)

ORIGIN: Madagascar
FAMILY: Liliaceae

RATING FOR HOME GROWTH: Easy

FLOWERING: Small white cluster.
LIGHT: Filtered light.
WATERING: Allow to partially dry before watering.
SOIL: Equal parts loam, sand, and peat moss.
PRUNING: Cut back only to produce multiple stems.

The dragon palm is a specimen plant which is important in home, office, and commercial decor, because of its tolerance to low light conditions. It is normally seen with multiple stems per pot, often with twisting or bending stems rather than erect.

Although it is fairly slow growing, the dragon palm does reach heights of 8' to 12'. The tall, slender stems are topped by terminal rosettes of 12" to 15" deep-green leaves that are about ½" wide. Cutting back the stems will cause the plant to branch.

There is a spectacular new variety of dragon palm, Dracaena marginata concinna, with variegated leaves. This tricolor version has its leaves striped with creams and reds in addition to green. Like the ordinary dragon palm, it too, is easy to grow.

DUMB CANE
(Dieffenbachia picta)

ORIGIN: Brazil
FAMILY: Araceae

**RATING FOR HOME
GROWTH:** Easy

FLOWERING: Greenish spathe surrounding slender spadix.
LIGHT: Filtered light.
WATERING: Keep on the dry side.
SOIL: Equal parts loam, sand, and peat moss.
PRUNING: None.

The beautiful foliage of dumb canes makes them extremely popular plants. People with children should be cautious, since all parts of this plant are toxic. Chewing on any part causes the tongue to swell up to such proportions that a person is rendered speechless, thus the name — "dumb" cane.

As these plants get older they have a tendency to lose their lower leaves. To rejuvenate your dumb cane, cut it off at the base. The plant will send up new shoots from the base. Cut off the bare interstem and the top may be rooted. The interstem can be cut into three inch sections and allowed to dry for two days. Then bury each section on its side, half way in a propagating mix. These sections will root and produce new plants.

EMERALD RIPPLE
(Peperomia caperata)

ORIGIN: Brazil
FAMILY: Piperaceae

RATING FOR HOME GROWTH: Easy

FLOWERING: Slender, greenish-white flower spikes.
LIGHT: Filtered light.
WATERING: Keep on dry side.
SOIL: Equal parts loam, sand, and peat moss.
PRUNING: None.

Forming a little rosette of heart-shaped, deeply crinkled leaves, the emerald ripple is probably the most widely grown of all peperomias. It is not a large plant, growing only about four inches tall with a spread of about five inches. For this reason it is a popular plant for terrarium use.

Overwatering is the major problem that is encountered in growing this plant. If you must make a mistake in watering this plant, make it on the dry side. The emerald ripple is propagated by rooting single leaves as with an African violet.

There is also a very rare form of this plant which has its leaves variegated with pale green and cream colors.

FIDDLELEAF FIG
(Ficus lyrata)

ORIGIN: Tropical Africa
FAMILY: Moraceae

RATING FOR HOME GROWTH: Easy

FLOWERING: Fig-like flowers.
LIGHT: Filtered light.
WATERING: Keep on the dry side.
SOIL: Equal parts loam, sand, and peat moss.
PRUNING: None.

Even after feeling the hard, leathery leaves of the fiddleleaf fig, it is difficult to believe that the plant is not artificial. The large, stately leaves of this plant are the most magnificent in the fig family. The fiddle-shaped leaves reach a size of 12″ to 18″.

Propagation can be accomplished by air layering. The first step in this method is to make a slit about 1/3 of the way into the stem at the point where it is desired that roots should form. Work some long-fibered moss into the incision and wrap a damp handful of the moss around the wound. Hold the moss in place by covering it with plastic film. Make sure the moss stays moist until the plant has rooted, then cut off the rooted portion and pot in soil.

FLUFFY RUFFLES FERN
(Nephrolepis exaltata 'Fluffy Ruffles')

ORIGIN: Variety of N. exaltata
FAMILY: Filices

RATING FOR HOME GROWTH: Easy

FLOWERING: None.
LIGHT: Filtered sun.
WATERING: Keep evenly moist, but not soggy.
SOIL: Equal parts loam, sand, peat moss, and leaf mold.
PRUNING: None.

Fluffy ruffles is a smaller and much slower growing variety of N. exaltata which is similar to the Boston fern. Bipinnate fronds give this fern a fluffy texture, hence the common name. The upright fronds of the fluffy ruffles fern grow to about 12″.

Care is basically the same as that for a Boston fern, however the fluffy ruffles is more susceptible to cold and drafts. Both plants are propagated in the same manner — by pinning the runners to the soil and allowing new plants to develop.

GREEN NEPHTHYTIS
(Syngonium podophyllum)

ORIGIN: Central America
FAMILY: Araceae

RATING FOR HOME GROWTH: Easy

FLOWERING: Spathe and spadix.
LIGHT: Filtered light.
WATERING: Keep evenly moist, but not soggy.
SOIL: Equal parts loam, sand and peat moss.
PRUNING: None, unless plant becomes leggy.

Among its merits, the green nephthytis is carefree and versatile. While young, this plant has thin arrow-shaped leaves and is a much used candidate in terrariums. As it grows older, the nephthytis becomes trailing or climbing. In its mature state it can then be used for hanging baskets or as a floor planter.

The green nephthytis, and old-fashioned plant, also has many variegated forms. All are relatively easy to care for. If a plant becomes leggy it does not object to being cut back hard. More light will usually prevent spindly growth. Propagate nephthytis species by stem-tip cuttings.

HOLLY FERN
(Cyrtomium falcatum)

ORIGIN: Asia, Hawaii
FAMILY: Filices

RATING FOR HOME GROWTH: Easy

FLOWERING: None.
LIGHT: Bright, filtered light.
WATERING: Keep evenly moist, but not soggy.
SOIL: Equal parts loam, sand, peat moss, and leaf mold.
PRUNING: None.

The shiny, leathery, dark green leaves of this plant are more typical of a Christmas holly than of a fern. The holly fern is unusual, but easy to grow. Tolerating some abuse, it is probably the hardiest of the indoor ferns. Like all ferns, it will benefit from occasional misting with distilled water.

Don't panic at the sight of small, round brown spots that will appear on the undersides of the leaves. These are not insects, but spores and indicate that the plant is healthy. Holly ferns can be propagated by the division of older plants, or the ambitious person may try propagation by spores.

IRON CROSS BEGONIA
(Begonia masoniana)

ORIGIN: China
FAMILY: Begoniaceae

**RATING FOR HOME
GROWTH:** Moderately easy

FLOWERING: Greenish-white flowers in spring.
LIGHT: Filtered light.
WATERING: Keep evenly moist, but not soggy.
SOIL: Equal parts loam, sand, and peat moss.
PRUNING: None.

The iron cross begonia is one of the most beautiful of all the begonias which are grown for their foliage. The white-hairy reddish stems are topped by light green leaves that are marked with brown-red iron crosses.

Propagation of iron cross begonias may be accomplished by means of leaf sections. Young plants will develop from the main veins on mature leaves after they are cut. Place the leaves on moist perlite and cut the primary veins. Pin down the leaves near the points of incision to keep the veins in touch with the propagating medium. Place whole set up inside a plastic bag to keep the humidity high and small plants will soon develop.

MAIDENHAIR FERN
(Adiantum cuneatum)

ORIGIN: Brazil
FAMILY: Filices

**RATING FOR HOME
GROWTH:** Difficult

FLOWERING: None.
LIGHT: Filtered light.
WATERING: Keep evenly moist; never allow to completely dry.
SOIL: Equal parts loam, sand, peat moss and leaf mold.
PRUNING: None.

The dainty and delicate appearance of the maidenhair ferns indicate the type of care which they require. All types of maidenhairs thrive in high humidity and are likely to suffer during the winter unless they are grown in a terrarium. Frequent misting with distilled water is also a help.

This variety of maidenhair is often grown by florists for use in floral arrangements. No other fern surpasses it for grace and beauty. It is too bad that the maidenhair fern does not easily become acclimated to the home. Propagation may be attempted by spores or by the division of older clumps.

NORFOLK ISLAND PINE
(Araucaria excelsa)

ORIGIN: Norfolk Island
FAMILY: Araucariaceae

RATING FOR HOME GROWTH: Easy

FLOWERING: None.
LIGHT: Sun to part sun.
WATERING: Keep evenly moist, but not soggy.
SOIL: Equal parts loam, sand, peat moss, and leaf mold.
PRUNING: None.

The Norfolk Island pine or star pine, as it is sometimes called, is a plant that is sure to attract attention. Many people are enchanted by the idea of having a living indoor Christmas tree and decorate their pines no matter what the size.

Norfolk pines are slow growing when young, but the growth rate picks up after the plants reach about three feet. The star-shaped arrangement of the branches is unique, but the plant will lose its symmetry if it only receives light from one direction. The pot should be rotated 180° every couple of days in order to prevent this.

Norfolk Island pines can be propagated from seeds if you can find a nursery which sells them.

PARLOR PALM
(Chamaedorea elegans 'bella')

ORIGIN: Guatemala
FAMILY: Palmae

RATING FOR HOME GROWTH: Easy

FLOWERING: Insignificant flowers on a light-yellow, branched spike.
LIGHT: Bright light, no sun.
WATERING: Keep evenly moist, but not soggy.
SOIL: Equal parts loam, sand, and peat moss.
PRUNING: None.

The parlor palm is a miniature palm which tolerates low light conditions. Because of its slow growth, this plant is a favorite for terrariums. Grown alone in pots, the parlor palm will eventually reach 18" to 24".

Watch for red spider mites which can infest this palm as well as others grown indoors. Speckling and discoloration of the leaf surface are signs that red spider mites have been sucking out vital plant juices. Frequent syringing of the palm with lukewarm water will help bring this problem under control.

Parlor palms may be easily propagated by removing the suckers which form around the main plant.

PONY-TAIL PALM
(Beaucarnea recurvata)

ORIGIN: Mexico
FAMILY: Liliaceae

**RATING FOR HOME
GROWTH:** Easy

FLOWERING: Panicles of small white flowers.
LIGHT: Sunny.
WATERING: Keep on the dry side.
SOIL: Equal parts loam, sand and peat moss.
PRUNING: None.

The rosette of thin linear leaves atop a large bulbous base gives the pony-tailed palm a fascinating appearance. Although the pony-tail can become a 30' tree in Mexico, it is extremely slow-growing indoors. As houseplants they are almost indestructible. They can last months without water and are not affected by low humidity. Specimens growing outdoors in Florida have even survived freezing temperatures.

As the pony-tail ages the base becomes larger. It almost looks as if the base had been covered with elephant skin which gives the plant its other common name of 'elephant's foot'. Usually, the larger the base the more valuable the plant. The larger plants are eagerly sought after since the pony-tail's growth rate is so slow.

PRAYER PLANT
(Maranta leuconeura kerchoveana)

ORIGIN: Brazil
FAMILY: Marantaceae

RATING FOR HOME GROWTH: Easy

FLOWERING: Small white flowers with purple streaks.
LIGHT: Filtered light.
WATERING: Keep evenly moist, but not soggy.
SOIL: Equal parts loam, sand, peat moss, and leaf mold.
PRUNING: None.

Without fail, the leaves of the prayer plant fold heavenward every evening, just as if they were hands in prayer. For this reason, they have been one of the oldtime favorites among indoor houseplants. The attractive foliage is dotted with reddish-brown spots running parallel to the main rib of each leaf.

Prayer plants adapt well to indoor culture, since they thrive in warm temperatures. Although they like moist soil, these plants should be kept slightly drier from December through February when they require somewhat of a rest period. Propagate prayer plants by cuttings or division of older plants.

RABBIT'S-FOOT FERN
(Davallia fejeenisis)

ORIGIN: Fiji Islands
FAMILY: Filices

RATING FOR HOME GROWTH: Moderately easy

FLOWERING: None.
LIGHT: Filtered light.
WATERING: Keep evenly moist, but not soggy.
SOIL: Equal parts loam, sand, peat moss and leaf mold.
PRUNING: None.

The amazing feature of the rabbit's-foot fern is not the foliage which is similar to carrot tops, but the surface rhizomes which bear a a remarkable resemblance to rabbits' feet. It is a good plant for moss-lined wire baskets which allow the best display of the odd-looking rhizomes.

Like other ferns, the rabbit's-foot will benefit from daily misting where low humidity is a factor. If possible use distilled water or rainwater to prevent a build-up of salts on the fronds.

Rabbit's-foot ferns may be propagated by cutting off sections of the rhizomes and rooting them on moist sphagnum moss covered with clear plastic.

RIBBON PLANT
(Dracaena sanderiana)

ORIGIN: Cameroons, Congo
FAMILY: Liliaceae

RATING FOR HOME GROWTH: Easy

FLOWERING: Insignificant clusters.
LIGHT: Filtered light.
WATERING: Keep evenly moist, but not soggy.
SOIL: Equal parts loam, sand, and peat moss.
PRUNING: Cut back to rejuvenate old plants.

The ribbon plant is a common houseplant which is relatively small and slow growing, at least for a dracaena. It is often used in terrariums and dish gardens for its leaf color which is gray-green with creamy-white margins. This color is especially showy in an arrangement with a background of green plants.

Another factor in the ribbon plant's favor is that it will tolerate most unfavorable conditions, except for cold. It even grows well in plain water and is a likely candidate for hydroponics.

Propagate the ribbon plant from stem cuttings as it becomes leggy.

RUBBER PLANT
(Ficus elastica 'Decora')

ORIGIN: India, Malaya
FAMILY: Moraceae

RATING FOR HOME GROWTH: Easy

FLOWERING: Fig-like flowers.
LIGHT: Sunny.
WATERING: Keep on the dry side.
SOIL: Equal parts loam, sand, and peat moss.
PRUNING: None.

As you can imagine from the name of this plant, the latex-bearing, milky sap which was once used to produce rubber, now is that of a striking accent plant in the home. This plant is so popular that each year acres upon acres of rubber plants are grown in Columbia for shipment to the United States.

Part of its appeal is due to the fact that it is so easy to care for. It tolerates low light conditions, however more light is necessary for optimum growth. Low light and overwatering are two factors that will quickly cause the rubber plant to loose its lower leaves. Frequent repotting is not necessary, as the rubber plant is quite happy with crowded roots.

SILVER TABLE FERN
(Pteris ensiformis 'Victoriae')

ORIGIN: Parent specie from Ceylon, Queensland, and Samoa
FAMILY: Filices

RATING FOR HOME GROWTH: Easy

FLOWERING: None.
LIGHT: Bright light, no direct sun.
WATERING: Keep evenly moist, but not soggy.
SOIL: Equal parts loam, sand, and peat moss.
PRUNING: None.

Table ferns comprise a large group of ferns with varying sizes and characteristics. Silver table fern ranks among the best of these. The silver-white fronds edged in dark green are uncommon among ferns.

This is one of the easier ferns to grow indoors, but like others it must not be allowed to dry out or placed too near a heat source. Since it only grows six to twelve inches tall, this has become a very popular terrarium plant. They can be propagated by spores or by gently pulling them apart at transplanting time.

SPIDER ARALIA
(Dizygotheca elegantissima)

ORIGIN: New Hebrides
FAMILY: Araliaceae

RATING FOR HOME GROWTH: Difficult

FLOWERING: Not in home.
LIGHT: Bright filtered or indirect.
WATERING: Keep evenly moist, but not soggy.
SOIL: Equal parts loam, sand, peat, and leaf mold.
PRUNING: Healthy plants which become leggy can have stalks. Cut back to desired level, new leaves will eventually sprout near point of cut.

Despite the difficulty in growing this graceful tropical shrub, it remains a popular house plant. Its long stalks are topped by leathery, dark green-almost black leaves. The thin leaflets become much wider as the plant matures.

Perhaps the main problem with growing the spider aralia is the low humidity of most homes in the winter. Misting the plant daily with distilled water may help alleviate the problem. It is also important to carefully watch the watering in the winter months. If the soil remains wet for long periods of time, the lower leaves of the plant are almost certain to fall off.

SPLIT-LEAF PHILODENDRON
(Monstera deliciosa)

ORIGIN: Mexico, Guatemala **RATING FOR HOME**
FAMILY: Araceae   **GROWTH:** Easy

FLOWERING: Spadix surrounded by a white spathe.
LIGHT: Filtered light.
WATERING: Keep evenly moist, but not soggy.
SOIL: Equal parts loam, sand, and peat moss.
PRUNING: None.

The split-leaf philodendron is probably the most popular large plant ever to be grown indoors. It is extremely easy to grow, but requires some special care to look its best. Probably the most important fact to remember is that even though this plant tolerates low light it requires brighter light in order for the leaves to split well and attain maximum size. Perforation and splitting also increase as the plant matures.

Do not remove the aerial roots which hang from the stems of the plant, just direct them into the pot. Propagate by rooting stem sections in damp sphagnum moss.

STAGHORN FERN
(Platycerium bifurcatum)

ORIGIN: E. Australia, New Guinea

FAMILY: Filices

RATING FOR HOME GROWTH: Moderately easy

FLOWERING: None.

LIGHT: Filtered sun.

WATERING: Keep evenly moist, but not soggy.

SOIL: Osmunda fiber; if not available use two parts long fiber sphagnum moss to one part sand, to one part leaf mold.

PRUNING: None.

To the plant lover, the staghorn is one of the most exciting of all ferns. The antler-shaped fertile fronds grow to three feet long, while the sterile roundish fronds are found at the base of the plant.

Staghorns are often sold mounted on a slab of rough wood or bark, but are almost impossible to care for indoors if grown this way. It is best to pot your staghorn fern in a clay pot with osmunda fiber or the potting mixture recommended above. This plant can be propagated with great patience from spores or by removing the small plants which form at the base of the mature ferns.

TSUS-SIMA FERN
(Polystichum tsus-simense)

ORIGIN: Korea
FAMILY: Filices

RATING FOR HOME GROWTH: Easy

FLOWERING: None.
LIGHT: Filtered light.
WATERING: Keep evenly moist, but not soggy.
SOIL: Equal parts loam, sand, peat moss and leaf mold.
PRUNING: None.

This little native of Korea is probably the best suited fern for terrarium growth. The dark green leathery fronds of this miniature fern rarely grow more than eight inches long. A two or three inch pot is adequate for this slow grower.

If not grown in a terrarium, the tsus-sima may have problems with the edges of the fronds turning brown. If this happens provide a higher humidity by misting the plant with distilled water and try to move it to a cooler location (68°-70° F). Older plants may be propagated by division.

UMBRELLA PLANT
(Cyperus alternifolius)

ORIGIN: Madagasgar
FAMILY: Cyperaceae

**RATING FOR HOME
GROWTH:** Easy

FLOWERING: Small, green flowers.
LIGHT: Filtered sun.
WATERING: Keep wet at all times.
SOIL: Equal parts loam, sand, and peat moss.
PRUNING: None.

Umbrella plants are perfect for the person who habitually overwaters his houseplants. It is impossible to give this plant too much water. (Do not confuse this plant with the umbrella tree — Brassia actinophylla). In fact it is often grown in a clay pot which is placed into a decorative ceramic pot filled to the top with water so that the entire clay pot is submerged.

Browning of the leaf tips may occur during the winter in homes with too low a humidity. Daily misting may help to discourage this. Brown leaves and even death will occur if the plant is allowed to get too dry.

The umbrella plant can be propagated by dividing the clumps it produces. Another method is by cutting off one of the umbrella-like tops with 2″ - 3″ of stem attached and rooting it in water or moist vermiculite.

UMBRELLA TREE
(Brassaia actinophylla)

ORIGIN: Australia
FAMILY: Araliaceae

RATING FOR HOME GROWTH: Easy

FLOWERING: 3′ spikes of red flowers.
LIGHT: Filtered sun.
WATERING: Keep on the dry side.
SOIL: Equal parts loam, sand, and peat moss.
PRUNING: None.

The umbrella tree is also commonly known as schefflera. As a small plant it really is not very exciting, but as it becomes larger the umbrella tree begins to assume the tropical elegance that it exhibits in its native state. Small plants are easily located and this is one of the fastest growing plants for indoor culture. A beautiful specimen can be grown in almost no time at all.

As one of today's most popular plants, the umbrella tree has few cultural problems. One problem to watch out for is red spider mites. They are mainly a problem in dry atmospheres. Frequent syringing with lukewarm water will help to alleviate the condition.

Propagate the umbrella tree by cuttings or from seeds.

UMBRELLA TREE

VARIEGATED PITTOSPORUM
(Pittosporum tobira 'Variegatum')

ORIGIN: China, Japan
FAMILY: Pittosporaceae

RATING FOR HOME GROWTH: Moderately easy

FLOWERING: Small white flowers.
LIGHT: Filtered sun.
WATERING: Keep on the dry side.
SOIL: Equal parts loam, sand, and peat moss.
PRUNING: Trim to shape.

These handsome evergreen shrubs are used extensively as landscaping material in California. Indoors, the variegated as well as the green pittosporum, become tough and durable plants. The variegated pittosporum has leathery, obovate leaves edged in creamy-white coloration.

Under indoor culture the pittosporum grow slowly, but steadily as long as sufficient light is present. The main problem that is likely to be encountered is the plants susceptiblity to red spider mite. This problem first shows up as a speckling and loss of leaf chlorophyll. If the infestation is heavy, minute webs can be seen on the underside of the leaves. About the only practical care is daily syringing of the plant with lukewarm water. Wet only the leaves, not the soil or root rot will likely develop.

WEEPING FIG
(Ficus benjamina)

ORIGIN: India, Malaya
FAMILY: Moraceae

**RATING FOR HOME
GROWTH:** Somewhat difficult

FLOWERING: Fig-like flowers.
LIGHT: Sunny.
WATERING: Keep on the dry side.
SOIL: Equal parts loam, sand, and peat moss.
PRUNING: None.

The graceful, arching branches of this small indoor tree make it a valuable indoor decorating item. Weeping figs are relatively slow growing plants so a specimen of any large size is a fairly expensive plant. Small plants are usually difficult to locate, but are reasonably priced.

The weeping fig has one disadvantage which may prevent it from being more popular than it is. This plant has the bad habit of producing many new leaves and then dropping them after it has been moved to a new location. Although this is a traumatic experience for many plant lovers, the weeping fig adjusts to its new location in time and stops dropping its leaves. Because of its beauty, the weeping fig is widely grown in spite of this problem.

Notes

Cacti and Succulents

Cacti and other succulents are among the most intriguing groups of plants grown in the home today. In addition to their unique appearances, cacti and succulents produce some of the showiest flowers among all plants.

The succulent stems of these plants are developed to withstand adverse climatic conditions so they are ideal candidates for indoor culture. Provide a few basic needs and these plants will grow indefinitely.

One of these needs is soil. Contrary to popular belief, cacti do not grow in pure sand. Their native soils are actually quite rich in organic matter and only fail to produce lush vegetation because of the lack of water. For this reason a cactus soil should contain 25% decayed leaf mold and humus. The rest of the mixture should be composed of 25% loam and 50% coarse sand.

Another misconception about cacti is that they never need water. A cactus in a pot outdoors needs a thorough watering twice weekly in the growing season. When brought indoors during the dormant season, the watering should be cut to once every two weeks. Of course, these watering schedules are dependent upon the soil being very porous. A heavy soil which remains moist can easily cause a succulent to rot.

Although most insects do not bother these plants, mealybug can become a troublesome pest. Malathion is the most common chemical control, but it is damaging to crassulas and living stones. One of the safest and most effective controls is to dip a cotton swab in rubbing alcohol and touch it to the mealybug. This may take patience and repetition, but this procedure will work.

Cacti, themselves, are easiest to multiply from cuttings. The cutting should be made with a sharp knife and then allowed to dry for several days, before it is placed in sand to root. Succulents other than cacti may be propagated in numerous ways. Many crassulas, kalanchoes, and sedums can be grown from single leaves. Stem cuttings is another method and the cuttings should be allowed to dry as with cacti. Both cacti and succulents can be seeded, but patience is required.

BIRDSNEST SANSEVIERIA
(Sansevieria trifasciata 'Hahnii')

ORIGIN: Sport of S. trifasciata laurentii

FAMILY: Liliaceae

RATING FOR HOME GROWTH: Easy

FLOWERING: Spike of small white flowers.
LIGHT: Filtered light (tolerates low light).
WATERING: Keep on dry side.
SOIL: Equal parts loam, sand, and peat moss.
PRUNING: None.

Birdsnest sansevierias are attractive and very undemanding plants. Their ease of care and ability to grow under unfavorable conditions, make them ideal office and home decorator plants. They are ideal for dish gardens and novelty planters.

This sansevieria is very slow growing. It forms a compact vase-like rosette which suckers freely. The plant can be propagated by removal of these suckers or by leaf cuttings.

There is also a beautifully, variegated form of the birdsnest sansevieria. This variety ('Golden hahnii') was produced in the 1950's and its leaves have golden marginal bands. Its only drawback is that at present it is a difficult plant to locate.

BISHOP'S CAP
(Astrophytum myriostigma)

ORIGIN: Central Mexico
FAMILY: Cactaceae

RATING FOR HOME GROWTH: Easy

FLOWERING: Large yellow flowers with a red throat
LIGHT: Sunny
WATERING: Keep on the dry side
SOIL: One part loam, one part leaf mold, and two parts sand
PRUNING: None

Although it is a cactus, the bishop's cap is not armed with any spines. Instead, the skin is so covered with silvery scales that the plant seems to have been sculptured out of grey rock. The plant is usually shaped with five conspicuous ribs, although the number is variable. The bishop's cap grows slowly up to 8″ in diameter.

Given enough light, the bishop's cap will produce large yellow flowers throughout the summer. This cactus is usually propagated from seed and is generally available at most garden centers, at least in the seedling size.

BUNNY EARS
(Opuntia microdasys)

ORIGIN: Mexico
FAMILY: Cactaceae

RATING FOR HOME GROWTH: Easy

FLOWERING: Light-yellow flowers
LIGHT: Sunny
WATERING: Keep on the dry side
SOIL: One part loam, one part leaf mold, and two parts sand
PRUNING: None

Bunny ears is a cute name for this cactus, but be careful not to touch it with bare hands. It is not covered with soft bunny-fur, but with very short bristles which can easily imbed themselves in the skin. They can be irritating and it is difficult to remove them all.

The common name for this cactus comes from the two new pads that grow near the "head" of an older pad. These pads are dotted with the little tufts of yellow bristles just mentioned. New cacti can be grown by removing (carefully) the pads and rooting them.

Watch the waterings of this cactus during the winter months. Bunny ears is very susceptible to rotting and should receive very little water and as much light as possible during this period.

BURRO'S TAIL
(*Sedum morganianum*)

ORIGIN: Mexico
FAMILY: Crassulaceae

RATING FOR HOME GROWTH: Easy

FLOWERING: Light-pink flowers
LIGHT: Sunny
WATERING: Keep on the dry side
SOIL: One part loam, one part leaf mold, and two parts sand
PRUNING: Not necessary

Burro's tail is perhaps the most beautiful of all sedums. A hanging basket with the branches dropping 2' to 3' over the sides is truly a sight to behold. Unfortunately, plants of this proportion are common only on the west coast. They are grown extensively in California, but cannot be packaged for shipping east. If shipping is attempted the plant is bound to lose most of its spindle-shaped leaves.

Because of the shipping problems, baskets of these plants are extremely expensive in the east. The best way to grow your burro's tail is to start with some small plants which are not hard to obtain. Any leaves that fall off can be used to propagate new plants. Starting off with a six-inch basket will produce the quickest results.

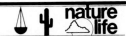

CHRISTMAS CACTUS
(Schlumbergera bridgesii)

ORIGIN: South America
FAMILY: Cactaceae

RATING FOR HOME GROWTH: Easy

FLOWERING: Drooping, light purple flowers with flared petals.
LIGHT: Filtered sun.
WATERING: Keep on the dry side.
SOIL: Equal parts loam, sand, peat moss, and leaf mold.
PRUNING: None.

The Christmas cactus is an oldtime favorite and probably the most popular of all flowering cacti. While easy to grow, this plant is often a reluctant bloomer. However, once a few cultural requirements are met, the Christmas cactus will provide its owner with a host of blossoms.

It should be understood that the Christmas cactus is a thermophotoperiodic plant. This means that its flowering is affected by temperature and light. The Christmas cactus is known as a short-day plant and will not initiate buds if it receives light for more than an 11 hr. period. High temperatures will result in inconsistent flowering, while too low temperatures (below 55°F) may inhibit flowering altogether. The optimum temperature range is 55°—70°F.

You can propagate your Christmas cactus by rooting stem pieces.

ELKHORN CACTUS
(Euphorbia lactea cristata)

ORIGIN: Species is from India
FAMILY: Euphorbiaceae

RATING FOR HOME GROWTH: Easy

FLOWERING: Will not flower in home
LIGHT: Sunny
WATERING: Keep on the dry side
SOIL: One part loam, one part leaf mold, and two parts sand
PRUNING: Remove normal branches that may occur

Cresting is a malformation that often occurs in cacti and succulents. This results in a twisted and unnatural growth. Although some growers shun these growths as being hideous, most collectors actively search for these forms.

The elkhorn cactus is the most popular of all the crested forms. It snakes, splits, wriggles, and fans into bizarre shapes. Too much water may encourage normal growth, so keep this plant dry.

Part of the reason for the rarity of the elkhorn is its slow growth pattern. A six inch plant can easily cost $10-$20 and larger sizes quickly escalate in price. Elkhorns can be propagated from cuttings, but they must callous over. Several days is usually all it takes before the cutting has dried enough to be planted in the propagating mix.

FISH-HOOK CACTUS
(Ferocactus acanthodes)

ORIGIN: So. California
FAMILY: Cactaceae

**RATING FOR HOME
GROWTH:** Easy

FLOWERING: 2" yellow or orange flowers
LIGHT: Sunny
WATERING: Keep on the dry side
SOIL: One part loam, one part leaf mold, and two parts sand
PRUNING: None

Ferocactus means 'ferocious cactus', which is a name justly deserved by this plant. The fierce reddish spines which cover the entire cactus, grow to 5" and are ready to hook on to anything that comes too close.

The wicked spines make the fish-hook cactus difficult to transplant without the shedding of a little blood. Use old newspaper folded several times into a belt and use this to hold on to the plant while repotting. This technique comes in handy when transplanting most cacti.

In the wild, the fish-hook cactus grows to be 9' tall. However, indoors growth is extremely slow and the plant will remain globular. Make sure your fish-hook gets as much sun as possible all year long.

FISHHOOK CACTUS

GOLDEN BARREL
(Echinocactus grusonii)

ORIGIN: Central Mexico
FAMILY: Cactaceae

**RATING FOR HOME
GROWTH:** Easy

FLOWERING: Yellow flowers in ring around the top of the plant
LIGHT: Sunny
WATERING: Keep on the dry side
SOIL: One part loam, one part leaf mold, and two parts sand
PRUNING: None

Consider yourself lucky if you own a specimen size golden barrel. Although this cactus can be easily grown from seed, it may take ten years to produce a 6″ plant. Mature specimens may become a globe that is one yard in diameter.

The golden-yellow spines highlight the green succulent flesh of this cactus. This combination is what makes the golden barrel stand out among other cacti.

The crown of the plant is covered with short golden wool. Here the flowers, and later the seeds are produced. The seed is hard to find in the U.S., since much of it is sold to Japan where the golden barrel is a valued plant.

GOLDEN STAR CACTUS
(Mammillaria elongata)

ORIGIN: Mexico
FAMILY: Cactaceae

**RATING FOR HOME
GROWTH:** Easy

FLOWERING: Cream-colored flowers
LIGHT: Sunny
WATERING: Keep on the dry side
SOIL: One part loam, one part leaf mold, and two parts sand
PRUNING: None

The golden star cactus forms 4" to 6" tall clustering cylinders. The golden star ranks high in popularity among cacti grown indoors and rightfully so. Each plant is covered with clusters of yellow interlacing spines, each one resembling a miniature starburst. The nature of these spines makes the golden star easier to touch than most cacti.

Given minimum care, the golden star can be counted on to display its little cream-colored flowers. Though they are not especially showy, its thrilling to see any cactus in bloom. Make sure to keep your golden star especially dry in the winter since it is very susceptible to rot at this time.

This cactus readily produces offsets. These can be removed and rooted to produce new plants. The golden star can also be grown from seed if available.

GOLF BALLS
(Epithelantha micromeris)

ORIGIN: Texas, N. Mexico   **RATING FOR HOME**
FAMILY: Cactaceae   **GROWTH:** Easy

FLOWERING: Pinkish-white flowers
LIGHT: Sunny
WATERING: Keep on the dry side
SOIL: One part loam, one part leaf mold, two parts sand
PRUNING: None

From a distance, this little cactus really does resemble a golf ball. They form tiny spheres, about one inch in size and are almost completely covered with dense, white spines. These spines are what give the golf ball cactus its unique appearance.

The small size of this plant makes it a favorite of cactus collectors. Unfortunately, golf ball is one of the rarer types of cacti. A factor contibuting to its rarity is its slow rate of growth. In time golf ball cacti form clumps which may be separated.

The little pinkish-white flowers of this plant are followed by red berries which provide another feature of attraction. If this plant is not obtainable at your local garden center, it can usually be mail ordered from the cactus growers in the southwest.

GRAFTED CACTI
(Gymnocalycium spp.)

ORIGIN: Mutations
FAMILY: Cactaceae

**RATING FOR HOME
GROWTH:** Moderately easy

FLOWERING: Yellow, red, or pink
LIGHT: Sunny
WATERING: Keep on the dry side
SOIL: One part loam, one part leaf mold, and two parts sand
PRUNING: Remove basal suckers

Mutations have resulted in many cacti with skins of vivid reds, yellows, pinks and oranges. Although they are pretty, these cacti cannot produce chlorophyll and would die if not grafted onto a green species. So, actually, these brightly colored cacti act as parasites on their host. The standards to which they are grafted manufacture food for both.

Species of gymnocalycium are not the only forms of cacti that are grafted. The first cactus in the picture is Chamaecereus silvestri lutea, the golden peanut cactus. Besides the colorful forms, many crested and other unusual cacti are grafted.

To grow these forms, extreme care must be exercised in watering during the winter months. The standard used for grafting is very susceptible to rot during the winter. It's also important to remove any green shoots which may sprout out of the stem or they may take over the entire plant.

IRISH MITTENS
(Opuntia vulgaris)

ORIGIN: Argentina
FAMILY: Cactaceae

**RATING FOR HOME
GROWTH:** Easy

FLOWERING: 3½″ yellow flowers
LIGHT: Sunny
WATERING: Keep on the dry side
SOIL: One part loam, one part leaf mold, and two parts sand
PRUNING: Only to control growth

Smooth, glossy, green pads give this rapid growing cactus its common name. Very few spines are produced on the smooth pads. Irish mittens is also one of the cacti known as a 'prickly pear', because of the red, pear-shaped fruit it produces. The fruit is about 3″ long and is edible.

Irish mittens really benefits from a summer out in the sun and will put on remarkable growth. Should the plant become too large, it can be pruned by removal of the pads at the joint. If allowed to callous over, these joint cuttings can be rooted to produce new plants.

There is also a variegated form of Irish mittens which is sometimes called "Joseph's coat cactus" (O. vulgaris variegata). The pads of this variety are splattered with white, yellow, and pink shades.

JADE PLANT
(Crassula argentea)

ORIGIN: S. Africa
FAMILY: Crassulaceae

RATING FOR HOME GROWTH: Easy

FLOWERING: Small, white star-shaped flowers
LIGHT: Sunny
WATERING: Keep on the dry side
SOIL: One part loam, one part leaf mold, and two parts sand.
PRUNING: None

The jade plant is probably the best liked of all succulents. It is a freely branching plant with thick fleshy pads for leaves. Much of its acceptance is due to the fact that it withstands all sorts of neglect, however it will become an outstanding specimen when grown under optimum conditions.

A summer vacation out on the patio will do wonders for this plant. Be sure that your jade is acclimated to the outdoors by leaving it out for short periods over a two week period. A shady spot under a tree is ideal for this, since a hot sun will burn the tender leaves. Once the plant has become used to the sun the leaves will take on a reddish glow and the jade may even cover itself with pinkish-white blossoms.

It has few insect enemies, but be on the watch for mealybug which seems to consider the jade plant a delicacy. Propagation may be accomplished by stem or leaf cuttings.

JELLY BEANS
(*Sedum rubrotinctum*)

ORIGIN: Mexico
FAMILY: Crassulaceae

**RATING FOR HOME
GROWTH:** Moderately easy

FLOWERING: Yellow flower clusters
LIGHT: Sunny
WATERING: Keep on the dry side
SOIL: One part loam, one part leaf mold, and two parts sand
PRUNING: Only to shape

This little succulent is often used as a ground cover and in rock gardens in southern California. The jelly-bean-like, succulent foliage is a shiny green with reddish tips. These tips become more red with increased light and this red and green coloration gives the plant its other common name of "Christmas cheer."

Because of its trailing habit, the jelly beans plant would probably look nice in a 6" hanging basket. Watch the water on this plant. The leaves quickly drop off with too much water or any other adverse condition.

Propagation is simple, as new plants will quickly develop from single leaves that are just laid upon the soil.

MEDICINE PLANT
(Aloe vera)

ORIGIN: Canary Islands
FAMILY: Liliaceae

RATING FOR HOME GROWTH: Easy

FLOWERING: Yellow flowers on a spike.
LIGHT: Sunny.
WATERING: Keep on the dry side.
SOIL: One part loam, one part leaf mold, and two parts sand.
PRUNING: None.

A number of aloes, such as this species, have been used since Greek and Roman times for medicinal purposes. Juice from the stem of the medicine plant is still used to heal burns. This is a handy plant to have on the kitchen windowsill. Aloe is also used commercially in the preparation of lotions to relieve sunburn.

The medicine plant grows as a freely suckering rosette. The gray-green leaves can grow from 16" to 22" in length. You can easily propagate your medicine plant by removing and potting up the suckers.

OLD MAN CACTUS
(Cephalocereus senilis)

ORIGIN: Mexico
FAMILY: Cactaceae

RATING FOR HOME GROWTH: Easy

FLOWERING: 2″ white flowers; night blooming.
LIGHT: Sunny.
WATERING: Keep on the dry side.
SOIL: One part loam, one part leaf mold, and two parts sand.
PRUNING: None.

Upright, columnar stems covered with long silver-white hairs make the old man cactus one of the most sought after of all cacti. Because of collectors, the 20′ to 40′ specimens that were once common in Mexico are now rare. Export of these plants is now controlled by the Mexican government. Plants now available are often sold at so much money per inch and plants over a foot tall are extremely expensive.

Seedlings of the old man are still available at reasonable prices so look for one of these. Don't look for flowers, since these cacti are usually about 20′ in their native state before they bloom. Since the plants are night-blooming, they are pollinated in a bizarre way — by vampire bats.

The old man is easy to care for, but make sure that it is rarely watered in the winter. An overdose could be fatal. Also a teaspoon of lime should be added to the soil mix.

OX-TONGUE CACTUS
(Gasteria verrucosa)

ORIGIN: South Africa
FAMILY: Liliaceae

RATING FOR HOME GROWTH: Easy

FLOWERING: Raceme of reddish flowers
LIGHT: Filtered sun
WATERING: Keep on the dry side
SOIL: One part loam, one part leaf mold, and two parts sand
PRUNING: None

As can quickly be seen by checking its family, the ox-tongue is not really a cactus, but a succulent member of the lily family. Like other members of this family, for example the aloes, and haworthias, the flowers are carried on a tall raceme.

The ox-tongue gets its name from the tongue-shape leaves. These leaves are covered with warty, white spots called tubercles. Cuttings may be taken from the leaves and used for propagation.

Removal of basal suckers is another method of starting new plants. The ox-tongue can also be grown from seed and many new hybrids have been produced in this manner.

PANDA PLANT
(Kalanchoe tomentosa)

ORIGIN: Madagasgar
FAMILY: Crassulaceae

RATING FOR HOME GROWTH: Easy

FLOWERING: White flowers with brown stripes.
LIGHT: Sunny.
WATERING: Keep on the dry side.
SOIL: One part loam, one part leaf mold, and two parts sand.
PRUNING: None

Like many members of this genus, the panda plant is also a native of Madagasgar. While it may grow to 2' in the wild, this plant is normally seen at 6" to 8" indoors.

The panda is a very attractive succlent with 3" long fleshy leaves. The main interest in the leaves is that they are covered with fuzzy white hairs. The tips of the leaves are coarsely toothed with the edges marked in brown.

The most amazing thing about the panda is the method in which it is propagated. This is accomplished by simply taking single leaves and laying them on the soil or moist sand. New plants will eventually emerge from each leaf.

nature life

PAPERSPINE CACTUS
(Opuntia turpinii)

ORIGIN: Argentina
FAMILY: Cactaceae

**RATING FOR HOME
GROWTH:** Easy

FLOWERING: Creamy-white flowers
LIGHT: Sunny
WATERING: Keep on the dry side
SOIL: One part loam, one part leaf mold, and two parts sand.
PRUNING: None

Opuntias comprise a group of cacti that vary in size from a few inches to over 15′ in height. They also vary in shape. The paperspine cactus is one of the most unusual and appealing members of the group. It is covered by odd, flat and papery spines which catch the immediate attention of any cacus lover.

The paperspine cactus forms a low spreading mound about 4″ high. The joints of this cactus are somewhat loosely attached and break loose rather easily. These joints can be rooted quite readily.

Flowering is extremely rare on the paperspine when grown indoors, probably from lack of light. As with other cacti, it is important to keep this one dry in the winter. A monthly watering should be sufficient.

PARTRIDGE BREAST
(Aloe variegata)

ORIGIN: South Africa
FAMILY: Liliaceae

RATING FOR HOME GROWTH: Easy

FLOWERING: Red flowers on a tall raceme
LIGHT: Sunny
WATERING: Keep on the dry side
SOIL: One part loam, one part leaf mold, and two parts sand
PRUNING: None

Aloes are favorite plants of many succulent collectors. Regrettably, most of the species are too large for indoor culture. Luckily, this is not the case with the partridge breast. This pretty, little succulent grows to be only 12″ high and 6″ across.

It is characterized by triangular, blue-green leaves that are streaked with linear white spots. This is the part of the plant that is supposed to resemble a partridge's breast.

This is one succulent that should flower readily if given enough light. It will not die back after flowering like some of the agaves. If the flowers are pollinized new plants may be grown from seed. Otherwise the partridge breast can be propagated by the removal of suckers which appear at the base of older plants.

PEANUT CACTUS
(Chamaecereus silvestrii)

ORIGIN: Argentina
FAMILY: Cactaceae

RATING FOR HOME GROWTH: Easy

FLOWERING: Large scarlet flowers
LIGHT: Sunny
WATERING: Keep on the dry side
SOIL: One part loam, one part leaf mold, and two parts sand
PRUNING: None

The little clusters of pale-green, peanut-shaped branches give this plant its common name. The branches are covered with short, white spines and break off easily. When removed these branches can be rooted to produce new plants.

It is very important to give the peanut cactus all the light possible in order to keep its shape. Under insufficient light conditions, the branches grow so thin and leggy that the plant becomes unrecognizable.

To produce flowers a cool dormant period in the winter is beneficial. The plant should receive plenty of sun and little water during this time. Given this treatment, the peanut cactus should bloom in May or June.

There is a grafted form of the peanut cactus, C. silvestrii lutea, that has beautiful yellow stems. This plant must be grafted onto another cactus, since it cannot produce its own food, because of a lack of chlorophyll.

PERUVIAN OLD MAN
(Espostoa lanata)

ORIGIN: Peru, Ecuador
FAMILY: Cactaceae

RATING FOR HOME GROWTH: Moderately easy

FLOWERING: Reddish flowers
LIGHT: Sunny
WATERING: Keep on the dry side
SOIL: One part loam, one part leaf mold, and two parts sand
PRUNING: None

When small, the Peruvian old man is completely covered with silvery hairs. As the plant grows taller, the hair on the lower stem may darken and wear off. This cactus is a very slow grower. It is rarely seen much taller than 2′ to 3′ although it does grow taller. Still, it is a much smaller plant than Cephalocereus senilis.

Although the Peruvian old man is basically columnar, it will sometimes be branching at the top. Give it as much sun as possible in the winter and be very careful with watering. Too much water at this time will cause rotting at the base of the cactus.

POWDER PUFF CACTUS
(Mammillaria bocasana)

ORIGIN: Mexico
FAMILY: Cactaceae

**RATING FOR HOME
GROWTH:** Easy

FLOWERING: Small creamy flowers.
LIGHT: Sunny.
WATERING: Keep on the dry side.
SOIL: One part loam, one part leaf mold, and two parts sand.
PRUNING: None.

The powder puff cactus is certainly a favorite among cacti in cultivation. This cactus flowers when very young and is also easily raised from seed. It is also a miniature type cactus which anyone can grow on their windowsill.

The powder puff forms 1½" to 2" clusters. The common name comes from the fact that the plant is covered with powder-white, silky hairs. Underneath the fluffy appearance are fishhook spines.

As the clumps become larger, they can easily be divided and the pieces rooted. A tablespoon of lime should be added to the potting mixture if possible.

PREGNANT PLANT
(Kalanchoe 'daigremontiana x tubiflora')

ORIGIN: Hybrid   **RATING FOR HOME**
(parents from Madagasgar) **GROWTH:** Easy
FAMILY: Crassulaceae

FLOWERING: Insignificant.
LIGHT: Sunny.
WATERING: Keep on the dry side.
SOIL: One part loam, one part leaf mold, and two parts sand.
PRUNING: Only if a branched plant is desired.

Pregnant plants could be termed the rabbits of the plant world, because of their rapid rate of reproduction. These plants have the curious habit of producing large numbers of little plantlets along the leaf margins of the parent plants. The baby plants easily drop off to produce a crowd of growing plants wherever they touch ground.

A glance at the picture will quickly reveal how the plant gets its other common name of chandelier plant. For obvious reasons, it is also known as the mother-of-thousands.

While your pregnant plant is relatively carefree, watch out for the cottony pest — mealy bug. Treat the problem in the usual manner, by cleaning with a cotton swab dipped in rubbing alcohol.

QUEEN VICTORIA AGAVE
(Agave victoria-reginae)

ORIGIN: Mexico
FAMILY: Amaryllidaceae

RATING FOR HOME GROWTH: Easy

FLOWERING: 10'-15' flower stalk with greenish flowers
LIGHT: Sunny
WATERING: Keep on the dry side
SOIL: One part loam, one part leaf mold, and two parts sand
PRUNING: None

The Queen Victoria agave certainly has a regal appearance. It forms a symmetrical rosette of stiffly, compressed leaves. These succulent leaves are 4" to 6" long with white edges and markings. The leaves end with a short spine.

The queen agave is very slow growing, so any large specimens have usually been collected in the wild. Most small plants have been grown from seed.

Besides the Queen Victoria agave, there is also a King Ferdinand agave. The king agave is similar, but forms a more open plant with fewer leaves. Although it is attractive, the king agave is rarely offered for sale.

RED FLOWERING CRASSULA
(Crassula schmidtii)

ORIGIN: S. W. Africa, Natal
FAMILY: Crassulaceae

RATING FOR HOME GROWTH: Easy

FLOWERING: Red flower clusters
LIGHT: Sunny
WATERING: Keep on the dry side
SOIL: One part loam, one part leaf mold, and two parts sand
PRUNING: Remove basal suckers

Occasionally used as a ground cover in southern California, this interesting crassula only grows to be 3" high. There are about 300 species of crassula and this is one of the better of the smaller types.

The coloring of the red flowering crassula is especially attractive. The leaves which are grayish-green on the topside are a handsome reddish color underneath. Of course, the red flower clusters are usually present to add to the effect.

This crassula like most others is propagated easily from stem cuttings.

SNAKE PLANT
(Sansevieria trifasciata)

ORIGIN: South Africa, Natal **RATING FOR HOME**
FAMILY: Liliaceae   **GROWTH:** Extremely easy

FLOWERING: Greenish-white flowers on a raceme
LIGHT: Tolerates low light
WATERING: Keep on the dry side
SOIL: Equal parts loam, sand, and peat moss
PRUNING: None

The only plant easier to grow than a snake plant is an artificial plant. It will grow in any part of the home that has a window in the same room. The more you neglect this plant, the happier it seems. However, a well grown plant will add accent to any home decor.

The erect, linear leaves grow 12″ to 18″ tall. They are dark green with bands of light green. In the variety S. trifasciata laurentii, the leaves are edged in gold bands which make them especially attractive.

Mother-in-law-tongue is another common name for this popular succulent. You can decide for yourself how the plant acquired this name.

The snake plant is easy to propagate. This can be done by dividing clumps of older plants or from leaf cuttings.

STAR CACTUS
(Astrophytum ornatum)

ORIGIN: Mexico   **RATING FOR HOME**
FAMILY: Cactaceae   **GROWTH:** Easy

FLOWERING: Light-yellow flowers
LIGHT: Sunny
WATERING: Keep on the dry side
SOIL: One part loam, one part leaf mold, two parts sand
PRUNING: None

The star cactus is often considered to be the most ornamental plant in its genus. Its succulent skin is attractively spotted with silvery scales, not quite as dense as on its cousin the bishop's cap cactus. Also unlike the bishop's cap, the star cactus is armed with long, sharp spines.

Although it will remain small under cultivation, the star cactus can grow up to 36" tall in its natural habitat. The 3½" yellow flowers are likely to be produced only in this plant's native state. Blossoming indoors is very unlikely to occur.

Star cacti like to have a little lime added to their soil. Give them plenty of light and a fair amount of water during the summer. Keep them cool and dry in the winter.

STARFISH CACTUS
(Stapelia gigantea)

ORIGIN: South Africa   **RATING FOR HOME**
FAMILY: Asclepiadaceae   **GROWTH:** Easy

FLOWERING: Giant 10″ to 15″ star-shaped flowers
LIGHT: Sunny
WATERING: Keep on the dry side
SOIL: Equal parts loam, sand, and peat moss
PRUNING: None

Although it's really neither a starfish nor a cactus, this bizarre plant does a good imitation of both. Since it is not a cactus, the four-ribbed stems are smooth and velvety. The flower is the part of this plant that mimics a starfish. The flowers are star-shaped and crossed with red lines.

Before the starfish cactus blossoms, it produces a large bud which looks like an inflated balloon. This bud, in turn, produces the large flower. The flower has an unpleasant odor, but it is not really bothersome unless you stick your nose into it. Since these plants are pollinated by flies, the flower produces a scent similar to rotting meat.

Because of the trailing habit of the starfish cactus, it can be grown in a hanging basket. This is also a good way to show off the blossoms which will hang over the end of the basket.

The starfish cactus can be propagated from dried stem cuttings.

TIGER JAWS
(Faucaria tigrina)

ORIGIN: S. Africa
FAMILY: Aizoaceae

RATING FOR HOME GROWTH: Easy

FLOWERING: Golden-yellow, daisy-like flowers.
LIGHT: Sunny.
WATERING: Keep on the dry side.
SOIL: One part loam, one part leaf mold, and two parts sand.
PRUNING: None.

Had this plant been discovered in 1975, it might simply have been called "Jaws" (after the shark motion picture). The menacing open jaws of this plant sport vicious looking "teeth" that are actually soft to the touch. This ferocious appearance makes tiger jaws an intriguing plant to both children and adults.

A surprising addition to the plant's beastly image are its magnificent yellow flowers. Their beauty turns this tiger into a pussycat. Unfortunately, they will not be produced unless adequate sunlight is provided.

Tiger jaws is a suckering plant and may be reproduced by removing the offsets. It can also be grown from seed if available.

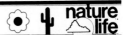

VARIEGATED CENTURY PLANT
(Agave americana 'Marginata')

ORIGIN: Mexico
FAMILY: Amaryllidaceae

RATING FOR HOME GROWTH: Easy

FLOWERING: 15' stalk with yellow flowers
LIGHT: Sunny
WATERING: Keep on the dry side
SOIL: One part loam, one part leaf mold, and two parts sand
PRUNING: None

Agave comes from the Greek word agavos which means admirable and that is a good word to describe this group of plants. They have a stately appearance and a regal air surrounding them. Most agaves make good houseplants in their juvenile stage.

The variegated century plant is one of the most striking of the agaves. It gets its common name from the idea that it takes 100 yrs. to blossom. Actually, the plant is usually mature enough to bloom after 10 yrs. under good conditions. The flower stem looks more like a telephone pole than a flower stalk. The tremendous effort needed to put forth such a flower takes its toll as the century plant dies after flowering.

Although the leaves can grow 4' to 5', the century plant will usually remain much smaller indoors. There is no need to worry about it blooming, but do be careful of the ends of the leaves which terminate in a vicious, spiny point.

ZEBRA HAWORTHIA
(Haworthia fasciata)

ORIGIN: South Africa
FAMILY: Liliaceae

**RATING FOR HOME
GROWTH:** Easy

FLOWERING: Small whitish flowers on a long, thin raceme
LIGHT: Filtered sun
WATERING: Keep on the dry side
SOIL: Equal parts loam, sand, and peat moss
PRUNING: None

This pretty, little succulent forms a 2″ to 3″ rosette of 2″ long upward curving leaves. These leaves are cross-banded with white, warty projections. Since it is not a large plant, the zebra haworthia is ideal for use in a succulent dish garden.

Providing it is not overwatered, the zebra haworthia is really an easy plant to grow. It even requires less light than most succulents and prefers to grow in filtered sun. A yearly fertilizing with house plant food diluted to half strength will suit this plant fine.

The easiest way to propagate this succulent is by the removal of the offsets which spring up from the parent plant.

Notes

Flowering and Colorful Foliage Plants

Growing conditions in the home are generally so poor that any plant which will flower indoors is sure to achieve instant acclaim. Just as popular are plants with colorful foliage that provide a change from the ordinary green of most plants. It is this attraction to flowers and color that makes these plants so popular even though many in this group are somewhat difficult to grow.

A general rule of thumb to follow in caring for plants is that flowering plants and plants with variegated foliage require more light than green plants. Many, such as the African violet, bloom under artifical lighting, but others such as Streptocarpus saxorum may never bloom without natural light. These preferences can be learned by trial and error.

Chrysanthemums, lilies, azaleas, poinsettias, and others like these belong to a group known as holiday plants. These flowering plants are not included in the following section, because they are not adapted to indoor culture. Instead, these are greenhouse crops meant to brighten the home for a few weeks and then be discarded. They can be coaxed into a second bloom with time and effort, but most home growers consider it not worth the toil. However, values can be relative, so don't be discouraged. If you want to accept the challenge, the task is possible.

Colorful foliage and flowering plants from crotons to orchids are eagerly being sought after by those tired of growing only philodendrons. This area of home horticulture is growing at the fastest pace and is the area to watch for the newest developments.

AFRICAN VIOLET

(*Saintpaulia ionantha 'var.'*)

ORIGIN: Tanzania
FAMILY: Gesneriaceae

RATING FOR HOME GROWTH: Moderately easy

FLOWERING: Single or double flowers in shades of lavender, pink, white or bicolor depending on the cultivar.
LIGHT: Bright filtered light.
WATERING: Keep evenly moist, but not soggy.
SOIL: Equal parts loam, sand, peat moss, and leaf mold.
PRUNING: None.

The first specimens of Saintpaulia ionantha were brought into the U.S. around the turn of the century. Since that time, the African violet has been bred to produce hundreds of varieties on its way to become the most popular of all flowering houseplants.

About 20 wild species are known today. These include miniature species and creeping or trailing types. However, almost all of the violets commonly grown are offspring of S. ionantha, which has single, light violet-blue flowers.

The care of African violets is easy, yet controversial, since many individual hobbyists claim contrary techniques. If a method of culture is working for you, continue to use it, but keep in mind the following facts about care.

1.) Violets will not tolerate cold. Cold water will leave spots on the foliage.
2.) Violets are sensitive to overwatering, which will cause roots to rot. Do not allow the plant to sit in a saucer of water.
3.) Light is probably the most important factor affecting bloom. Given enough light, violets will bloom constantly, however avoid a scorching sun.
4.) During active growing periods, feed often with a weak liquid fertilizer.

32-301-10

ALUMINUM PLANT
(Pilea cadierei)

ORIGIN: Vietnam
FAMILY: Urticaceae

**RATING FOR HOME
GROWTH:** Easy

FLOWERING: Insignificant greenish flower clusters.
LIGHT: Filtered light.
WATERING: Keep evenly moist, but not soggy.
SOIL: Equal parts loam, sand, and peat moss.
PRUNING: Pinch growing tip frequently to encourage branching.

At one time, the aluminum plant was probably the most popular species of all pileas. Now, new hybrids have come along to charm their way into people's homes, but the aluminum plant still remains a good seller. Plated with a silver-grey aluminum cast over green leaves, this plant has a unique color which sets it apart from others.

Besides being a pot plant, its best use is probably in terrariums. There is a variety, P. cadierei 'Minima', which is a slower growing dwarf form. This variety adapts especially well to terrarium culture. Either form is easily propagated by stem-tip cuttings.

AMARYLLIS
(Hippeastrum spp.)

ORIGIN: Tropical America   **RATING FOR HOME**
FAMILY: Amaryllidaceae   **GROWTH:** Easy

FLOWERING: Large, trumpet-shaped flowers
LIGHT: Sunny
WATERING: Keep on the dry side
SOIL: Equal parts loam, sand, and peat moss
PRUNING: None

An amaryllis is probably the most popular of all bulbous plants grown by the indoor gardener. Bulbs are usually offered for sale in December that will blossom in January or February. The new hybrids will produce flowers 8" to 10" across. Well-grown bulbs will usually send up a stalk topped by 3 or 4 flowers, followed by a second stalk as the first begins to fade.

After the flowers have withered, the hollow stems should be cut back to the base of bulb. Strap-like green leaves will appear and normal watering should take place. If possible, the amaryllis should be placed outdoors for the summer and fertilized monthly. In September, water should gradually be withheld, the plants brought indoors and allowed to go dormant. If possible, the dormant bulb should be placed in a cool location.

Around January, a new flower bud should begin to show. Watering should gradually be started at this time. Give the amaryllis plenty of light during this period. Since the flower stalk is hollow and the flowers so large, it is probably a good idea to stake the stalk. This will prevent the disappointment of a broken flower stem.

ANGELWING BEGONIA
(*Begonia lucerna*)

ORIGIN: Hybrid
FAMILY: Begoniaceae

RATING FOR HOME GROWTH: Easy

FLOWERING: Large clusters of drooping pink flowers
LIGHT: Filtered light
WATERING: Keep evenly moist, but not soggy
SOIL: Equal parts loam, sand, and peat moss
PRUNING: To promote branching

Angelwing begonias were among grandmother's favorite plants and they are still popular today. There are many varieties with different size and color in the leaves. Most of these varieties will bloom with pendulous flower clusters. Some of these clusters may have as many as 20 to 30 flowers.

Angelwings are sometimes grown in hanging baskets, but they have a tendency to grow more upright, so they may have to be cut back. This is also true of angelwings in pots, since they also have a tendency to become leggy.

The leaves of the angelwing begonia are covered with silvery-white spots. These spots make the plant attractive even when not in bloom. The angelwing is happy in the bright light of either an east or west window. Too much direct sun will burn the leaves.

BIRD OF PARADISE
(Strelitzia reginae)

ORIGIN: S. Africa
FAMILY: Musaceae

RATING FOR HOME GROWTH: Easy

FLOWERING: Exotic orange and blue flowers.
LIGHT: Sunny.
WATERING: Allow to partially dry before watering.
SOIL: Equal parts loam, sand, and peat moss.
PRUNING: None.

The banana-shaped leaves of the bird of paradise are not especially appealing, but promise of future flowers endears this plant to many green-thumbers. A certain amount of patience is required to get this plant to blossom.

The bird of paradise probably will not bloom until the plant has produced at least ten leaves, which may take from three to five years. Flowers are also more likely to be produced if the plant becomes pot bound, so frequent transplanting is unnecessary. A summer outdoors on the patio would also be beneficial to this plant.

New plants can be produced by division of older specimens.

CAPE PRIMROSE
(Streptocarpus rexii)

ORIGIN: S. Africa
FAMILY: Gesneriaceae

RATING FOR HOME GROWTH: Easy

FLOWERING: Lavender, trumpet-like flowers.
LIGHT: Filtered light.
WATERING: Allow to slightly dry before watering.
SOIL: Equal parts loam, sand, peat moss, and leaf mold.
PRUNING: None.

The spectacular blooms of the cape primrose attract immediate attention. The large trumpet-like flowers are some of the showiest for a member of the African violet family. The flowers are completed by quilted fuzzy, long narrow leaves in a low growing rosette.

Remember to cut the old flower stems as soon as the blossoms have faded. This way more of the plant's strength can be diverted into flower production without having to produce seed. The cape primrose begins to blossom in early spring and with care blooms will be produced well into fall.

Propagation can be accomplished by one of three methods. Old clumps may be divided, new plants may be started from single leaves, or plants may be grown from seed.

CHRISTMAS KALANCHOE
(Kalanchoe blossfeldiana 'Tom Thumb')

ORIGIN: Madagasgar
FAMILY: Crassulaceae

RATING FOR HOME GROWTH: Easy

FLOWERING: Bright red clusters of flowers.
LIGHT: Sunny.
WATERING: Keep on dry side.
SOIL: Equal parts loam, sand, and peat moss.
PRUNING: None.

Recently, the flowering types of kalanchoes have become very popular. The new hybrids put on a showy exhibition of colorful bloom. Since they are succulents, these plants are not bothered by low humidity.

Kalanchoes are photoperiodic plants which means that their blooming is dependent upon daylength. The normal blossomtime is from Jan. to Feb., but they can be brought into bloom in any season by covering them with black cloth or plastic and limiting daylength to nine hours, until flower buds are showing.

Propagate kalanchoes by rooting leaves in the same manner as African violets.

CROSSANDRA
(Crossandra infundibuliformis)

ORIGIN: India
FAMILY: Acanthaceae

RATING FOR HOME GROWTH: Easy

FLOWERING: Spikes of orange flowers.
LIGHT: Filtered light.
WATERING: Keep evenly moist, but not soggy.
SOIL: Equal parts loam, sand, peat moss and leaf mold.
PRUNING: Pinch to keep from getting leggy.

The shiny, oval, dark green foliage of the crossandra would be attractive even if it were not complimented by the showy spikes of orange flowers. It is a slow grower up to 8″ or 12″ with the flower often overshadowing the plant.

Insects are rarely a problem, although scale, whitefly, and aphids will attack the plant if they are in the area.

Besides propagation from cuttings the crossandra is also easy to germinate from seeds. A seedling will flower within a few months time.

CROWN OF THORNS
(Euphorbia splendens)

ORIGIN: Madagasgar
FAMILY: Euphorbiaceae

RATING FOR HOME GROWTH: Easy

FLOWERING: Salmon-red flower bracts.
LIGHT: Filtered sun.
WATERING: Keep on dry side.
SOIL: Equal parts loam, sand, and peat moss.
PRUNING: Pinch terminal growth to develop branching.

Reddish flower bracts combine with the small flowers on the crown of thorns to produce a pleasing display. Given enough light, this plant will be practically everblooming.

The long, rather thin branches of the plant are armed with intimidating thorns. These branches are not strong enough to remain upright and should have some support.

Crown of thorns is a xerophytic plant, which means that it is adapted to withstand long periods of drought. However, the leaves will fall off if the plant is allowed to remain dry too long. Do not become alarmed if this should happen, simply resume normal care and the plant will respond with a new set of leaves.

FALSE HEATHER
(Cuphea hyssopifolia)

ORIGIN: Mexico, Guatemala **RATING FOR HOME**
FAMILY: Lythraceae   **GROWTH:** Easy

FLOWERING: Small lavender flowers.
LIGHT: Sunny.
WATERING: Keep evenly moist, but not soggy.
SOIL: Equal parts loam, sand, and peat moss.
PRUNING: Pinch to create a bushier plant.

Anytime an easy to grow plant will flower indoors it is certain to become a favorite. Given enough light, the false heather will almost be in constant bloom. Although each flower is small, a number scattered over the plant is an impressive sight.

The false heather is not a large plant, growing only about 12" to 18". It tolerates low light conditions, but some sun is necessary to keep it in bloom. Propagate it by stem-tip cuttings.

FANCY-LEAVED CALADIUM
(Caladium hortulanum)

ORIGIN: Tropical America
FAMILY: Araceae

**RATING FOR HOME
GROWTH:** Moderately
difficult

FLOWERING: Spathe and spadix; not showy
LIGHT: Filtered light
WATERING: Keep evenly moist, but not soggy
SOIL: Equal parts loam, sand, peat moss and leaf mold
PRUNING: None

The strikingly beautiful foliage of the caladium makes it a commonly grown houseplant, even though it can be difficult to raise. Caladium bulbs are usually offered for sale in the winter, since they go through a dormancy just like the amaryllis.

The most important cultural fact to remember in the raising of caladiums is that the delicate leaves are very sensitive to cold. The plant should be kept warm at all times. Even air conditioning is harmful to the caladium.

In late fall the foliage should be allowed to die, so that the plant can have a rest period. Older plants can be propagated by dividing the tubers, before the caladium is brought out of dormancy.

FLAMINGO FLOWER
(Anthurium scherzerianum)

ORIGIN: Costa Rica
FAMILY: Araceae

**RATING FOR HOME
GROWTH:** Moderately easy

FLOWERING: Coiling spadix, brilliantly colored spathe
LIGHT: Filtered light
WATERING: Keep evenly moist, but not soggy
SOIL: Equal parts shredded bark, coarse leaf mold and sand
PRUNING: None

Most indoor gardeners classify anthuriums as exotic tropicals not to be grown in the home. Happily, this is untrue and the flamingo flower can be grown inside with little difficulty.

The flamingo flower does not vine like some of the anthuriums. Instead, it produces good compact growth reaching about 12″ high. The spathes are as brightly colored as any anthurium. They come in glowing shades of red, pink salmon, and even white with red dots. Flowering takes place throughout most of the year and individual flowers are long-lasting.

Low humidity is the main factor in the failure of anthuriums. Frequent misting may help. Bright light is also necessary, but direct sun will burn the leaves.

FRECKLEFACE
(Hypoestes sanguinolenta)

ORIGIN: Madagasgar
FAMILY: Acanthaceae

RATING FOR HOME GROWTH: Easy

FLOWERING: Small lavender flowers
LIGHT: Filtered sun
WATERING: Keep evenly moist, but not soggy
SOIL: Equal parts loam, sand, peat moss, and leaf mold
PRUNING: Constant pinching to keep plant from getting too leggy

Freckleface seems to be one of those plants that you either like or just do not like at all. It's most redeeming quality is the dull green leaves that are splashed with pink dots. The freckleface may grow from 1' to 2' tall but must be constantly cut back or it will be leggy with the leaves spaced far apart.

This plant will blossom, but the flowers are not spectacular. For some unexplained reason, the plant appears to go semi-dormant after flowering. There have been reports of it dying back to the ground and later resprouting.

The new leaves of the Freckleface are covered with fine white hairs which disappear as they become older. The amount of "freckles" seems to depend on the amount of light that the plant receives. The more light that the plant receives, the more spots the leaves will produce.

GARDENIA
(Gardenia jasminoides)

ORIGIN: China
FAMILY: Rubiaceae

**RATING FOR HOME
GROWTH:** Moderately
difficult

FLOWERING: Fragrant, 2″ to 3″ double, white flowers
LIGHT: Sunny
WATERING: Keep evenly moist, but not soggy
SOIL: Equal parts loam, sand, and peat moss
PRUNING: To shape as desired

The heavy fragrance of a gardenia blossom can scent an entire room. These double, white flowers have long been a favorite for corsages on special occasions. Besides the aromatic blooms, the gardenia is covered with handsome glossy-green foliage. The attributes of the gardenia seem almost too good to be true, unfortunately, this plant is somewhat difficult to grow.

One problem is chlorotic leaves when the soil is too alkaline. This is not serious and can be corrected through the use of an acid fertilizer. The most serious problem is that the gardenia often drops its flower buds before they open. This is usually because of nighttime temperatures.

A gardenia will not set buds if night temperatures are over 65° F. or under 55° F. Once the buds have been set, temperatures over 70° F. may cause them to drop. Although the gardenia is a little tempermental, it is definitely worth any extra effort it takes to grow this spectacular plant.

GLOXINIA
(Sinningia speciosa 'var.')

ORIGIN: Brazil, hybrids
FAMILY: Gesneriaceae

RATING FOR HOME GROWTH: Moderately easy

FLOWERING: 3" to 5", bell-shaped flowers
LIGHT: Filtered light
WATERING: Keep evenly moist, but not soggy
SOIL: Equal parts loam, sand, peat moss, and leaf mold
PRUNING: None

There are many varieties of gloxinias with outstanding flowers. The 3" to 5" blooms make the gloxinia one of the more popular gift plants. Unlike most holiday plants, the gloxinia can be kept to bloom year after year.

Gloxinia bulbs are usually available for sale in late winter. If started then, they can be counted on to bloom through most of the summer. After flowering is complete, the foliage will die down. Watering should then be stopped and the plant left dormant. After its resting period, the gloxinia can be put in bright light and watering can gradually resume.

Besides being grown from bulbs, gloxinias can also be propagated from seed and from leaf cuttings.

GLOXINIA

GOLD-DUST DRACAENA
(Dracaena godseffiana)

ORIGIN: Zaire
FAMILY: Liliaceae

**RATING FOR HOME
GROWTH:** Moderately easy

FLOWERING: Greenish-yellow flowers.
LIGHT: Filtered light.
WATERING: Keep evenly moist, but not soggy.
SOIL: Equal parts loam, sand and peat moss.
PRUNING: Pinch to keep full.

New foliage on the gold-dust dracaena is a shiny green and looks as if someone had splattered it with yellow paint. Later on these yellow spots mature to white.

The gold-dust dracaena is one of the more popular plants in the genus and is actually a member of the lily family. Since it is slow growing, it finds its chief uses in dish gardens and terrariums.

There is a variety of gold-dust dracaena named 'Florida beauty' which is also very popular. The leaves of this form are covered with so much creamy-white variegation, that little can be seen of the deep green color.

GOLD-SPOT EUONYMUS
(Euonymus japonicus medio-pictus)

ORIGIN: Japan
FAMILY: Celastraceae

**RATING FOR HOME
GROWTH:** Moderately easy

FLOWERING: Tiny greenish-white flowers.
LIGHT: Sunny.
WATERING: Keep evenly moist, but not soggy.
SOIL: Equal parts loam, sand, and peat moss.
PRUNING: Pinch growing tips to encourage branching.

Dark-green oval leaves with bright-yellow centers make the gold-spot euonymus a stunning foliage plant. Indoors it is extremely slow growing and will need a large pot very infrequently.

The gold-spot euonymus is a semi-hardy broadleaf evergreen which may survive outdoors as far north as lower Michigan if given a sheltered area during the winter.

This plant does have two problems which must be carefully watched. One is that it is prone to mildew attack and needs good air circulation under damp conditions to prevent the disease. The other problem is that of red spider mites, which will attack the plant under dry conditions. Frequent syringing with lukewarm water will discourage the mites.

HIBISCUS
(Hibiscus rosa-sinensis)

ORIGIN: Tropical Asia
FAMILY: Malvaceae

RATING FOR HOME GROWTH: Easy

FLOWERING: Large flowers with wavy petals and a long red staminal column with yellow anthers.
LIGHT: Sunny.
WATERING: Keep evenly moist, but not soggy.
SOIL: Equal parts loam, sand, and peat moss.
PRUNING: Trim to shape.

The exotic appearance of a hibiscus blossom will excite any plant lover. Though the blooms only remain open for one day and then die, the plant is practically everblooming.

Your hibiscus should be placed out on the patio for a summer vacation. During this time it will need lots of water and fertilizer and will reward you with almost constant flowering. It should then be taken indoors in the fall and cut back about 1/3 for a winter rest.

New plants may be started from cuttings taken in the spring. Hibiscus flowers come in color shades of red, pink, yellow and orange. There is also a variety with double flowers which also comes in various colors.

JERUSALEM CHERRY
(Solanum pseudo-capsicum)

FAMILY: Solanaceae

RATING FOR HOME GROWTH: Easy

FLOWERING: Starry white flowers, followed by cherry-like fruit.
LIGHT: Sunny.
WATERING: Allow to slightly dry before watering.
SOIL: Equal parts loam, sand, and peat moss.
PRUNING: None.

Also known as Christmas cherry, this old favorite seems to have lost much of its holiday demand to the poinsetta. The Jerusalem cherry seems to be on its way to becoming a year-round plant. It can even be grown outdoors as an annual if the seeds are started in late winter indoors.

This plant is a member of the nightshade family which contains valuable food crops such as tomatoes, potatoes, and eggplant. The night-shade family also includes many members which are deadly poison, so remember that even though the Jerusalem cherry looks tempting, it is not edible.

This plant is very attractive to whitefly so keep a close watch for the insects and their eggs on the underside of the leaves. Propagate the Jerusalem cherry from seed or stem cuttings.

KAFIR LILY
(Clivia miniata)

ORIGIN: Natal
FAMILY: Amaryllidaceae

**RATING FOR HOME
GROWTH:** Easy

FLOWERING: Tall stems with clusters of scarlet flowers with yellow throats.
LIGHT: Filtered sun
WATERING: Keep on the dry side
SOIL: Equal parts loam, sand, and peat moss
PRUNING: None

The leathery, dark-green, strap-like leaves of the kafir lily are very similar to those of the amaryllis. One of the differences between these two plants is that the kafir lily does not go completely dormant in the fall. Instead it has a resting period. Reduce water at this time, but make sure that the leaves do not wilt.

The kafir lily puts out its beautiful flower stems between March and May. During this period of active growth and all summer the kafir lily will use a lot of water, and lots of plant food. Fertilizer should be given at regular monthly intervals during the growing season.

Kafir lilies are easy plants to grow from seed, but it will then take several years for them to blossom. Large plants may be divided as they fill up their containers.

MINIATURE ORANGE
(Citrus mitis)

ORIGIN: Madeira
FAMILY: Rutaceae

RATING FOR HOME GROWTH: Moderately difficult

FLOWERING: White, fragrant flowers
LIGHT: Sunny
WATERING: Allow to slightly dry before watering
SOIL: Equal parts loam, sand, and peat moss
PRUNING: To shape the plant

One of the most fascinating sights in the indoor garden is a miniature tree that is loaded with fruit and flowers. For this reason, the miniature orange has been a disappointment to the many amateurs who have bought it and not realized the type of care it required.

First of all, a sunny location is absolutely needed for a healthy citrus plant. Secondly, the right amount of water is important. Overwatering will cause the leaves to shrivel and drop from the plant. Let the miniature orange slightly dry and then make sure to give it a thorough watering. A monthly fertilizing with an acid fertilizer is also helpful.

Red spider mites and scale insects seem to be especially fond of this plant. Frequent misting and an occasional preventative spraying with an indoor insecticide will help to discourage these pests.

Given the proper care, the miniature orange will reward its owner with fragrant blossoms throughout the year. When pollinizing insects are not present the flowers can be fertilized with a little brush or by touching one flower to another. The little orange fruits that are produced are slightly bitter, but completely edible.

MOON VALLEY PILEA
(Pilea 'Moon Valley')

ORIGIN: New variety
FAMILY: Urticaceae

RATING FOR HOME GROWTH: Easy

FLOWERING: Conspicuous clusters of greenish-white flowers.
LIGHT: Filtered light.
WATERING: Keep evenly moist, but not soggy.
SOIL: Equal parts loam, sand, and peat moss.
PRUNING: None.

The moon valley pilea has rapidly become one of the most popular of all pileas. The deeply quilted ovate leaves and the reddish-brown coloration along the main veins are extra-attractive when combined with the light nile-green color of the foliage.

Since it is freely branching, the moon valley pilea makes an ideal pot plant. However, like many pileas it adapts very well to terrarium culture, where the clusters of small flowers draw attention as well as the beautiful foliage. Propagate this plant in the same manner as other pileas, by stem-tip cuttings.

259

MRS. HENRY COX GERANIUM
(Pelargonium x hortorum 'Mrs. Henry Cox')

ORIGIN: Hybrid
FAMILY: Geraniaceae

RATING FOR HOME GROWTH: Moderately easy

FLOWERING: Single, salmon flowers
LIGHT: Sunny
WATERING: Keep on the dry side
SOIL: Equal parts loam, sand, and peat moss
PRUNING: Pinch to keep full

Mrs. Henry Cox is a geranium that thinks it is a coleus! The circular leaf zones of pinks, creams, and greens are certainly more typical of coleus color than of geranium leaves. These amazing tones make this tricolor geranium appealing even when not in bloom. The beautiful foliage compensates for what Mrs. Henry Cox lacks in blossoms. The single flowers are not as attractive as other geranium flowers.

Mrs. Cox is fairly easy to care for, except it must be watched in the winter. During this time it must receive as much light as possible. Geraniums also appreciate cooler temperatures, between 65° F. and 70° F. would be perfect. Geraniums also like to be kept on the dry side, especially in the winter.

Propagate any of your geraniums by stem cuttings.

NERVE PLANT
(Fittonia verschaffeltii argyroneura)

ORIGIN: Peru
FAMILY: Acanthaceae

RATING FOR HOME GROWTH: Difficult

FLOWERING: Small yellow flowers.
LIGHT: Filtered light.
WATERING: Keep evenly moist, but not soggy.
SOIL: Equal parts loam, sand and peat moss.
PRUNING: Pinch to keep full.

Although it is often used in hanging baskets in Florida and California, the nerve plant will not grow well indoors because it will not tolerate dry air. This does not mean it cannot be grown, but its use is confined to terrariums where it puts on a brilliant display.

The 2″ to 4″ oval leaves are a vivid green, prominently veined with a white nerve network. There is also another form, F. verschaffeltii with deep-red veins. Either form can be propagated by stem-tip cuttings.

PINEAPPLE PLANT
(Ananas comosus)

ORIGIN: Brazil
FAMILY: Bromeliaceae

RATING FOR HOME GROWTH: Easy

FLOWERING: Bright purple flowers, colored bracts, followed by fruit.
LIGHT: Sunny.
WATERING: Allow to dry slightly between waterings.
SOIL: Equal parts loam, sand, peat and leafmold, or well drained commercial mix.
PRUNING: None.

The pineapple plant makes an interesting conversation piece, since it is usually sold while bearing fruit. The plant itself forms a large terrestrial rosette 30 to 36 inches high with spiny-edged, dull-grey leaves.

If this plant is not available from local nurseries, try the nearest supermarket. Simply slice off the rosette of leaves from the top of a ripe pineapple fruit. Allow this top to dry for several days and plant with the base about 1″ deep in moist soil. If your pineapple roots, it can be induced to fruit after 18 months to 2 years. This can be accomplished by quartering an apple, placing the pieces around the base of the plant, and covering the plant with plastic. The ethylene gas produced by the apple will provide the stimulus for the pineapple to fruit.

REX BEGONIA
(Begonia rex)

ORIGIN: Hybrids
FAMILY: Begoniaceae

**RATING FOR HOME
GROWTH:** Moderately
Difficult

FLOWERING: Small, rose-colored flowers
LIGHT: Filtered light
WATERING: Keep evenly moist, but not soggy
SOIL: Equal parts loam, sand, peat moss, and leaf mold
PRUNING: None

Beautifully brocaded foliage makes these plants the most favored of all the begonias. There are hundreds of varieties of rex begonias, each with its unique color combinations. The flowers of these plants are not especially showy, but the leaf tones more than compensate. 'Merry Christmas' with its red, white, and green leaves is a popular variety.

Rex begonias are good plants for a north window, since direct sun can burn the leaves. The leaves are also prone to mildew attack. If this occurs, it can best be controlled by the application of a systemic fungicide.

Most varieties of rex begonia like a resting period during the winter. Decrease the water amounts and stop all fertilizing during this period. Rex begonias can be propagated from leaf section cuttings.

SHRIMP PLANT
(Beloperone guttata)

ORIGIN: Mexico
FAMILY: Acanthaceae

RATING FOR HOME GROWTH: Easy

FLOWERING: White flowers and reddish-brown bracts.
LIGHT: Sunny.
WATERING: Keep on the dry side.
SOIL: Equal parts loam, sand and peat moss.
PRUNING: Pinch often to keep from getting leggy.

With its shrimp-like flowers, the shrimp plant is an attraction to almost everyone who sees it. This plant is almost everblooming with enough light and begins blooming at a very early age. While the plant is small, flower buds should be removed. This practice should continue, until the plant has reached its desired height, otherwise it will be weakened by constant blooms.

A monthly fertilizing with any good houseplant food will help encourage foliage and improve the overall appearance of your shrimp plant. It can be propagated by stem-tip cuttings.

SILVER TREE
(Pilea 'Silver Tree')

ORIGIN: Caribbean
FAMILY: Urticaceae

RATING FOR HOME GROWTH: Easy

FLOWERING: Tiny, greenish flower clusters
LIGHT: Filtered light
WATERING: Keep evenly moist, but not soggy
SOIL: Equal parts loam, sand, and peat moss
PRUNING: Pinch to keep bushy

The pileas are a well-liked group of plants. Although their flowering is insignificant, their usefullness and easy culture is appealing. The silver tree is one of the most popular of the pileas.

The silver tree is not a large plant. Its dark leaves are accented by a silver band along their center. There are little silver dots to each side of this band.

Because of the colorful leaves, the silver tree is a popular plant for terrariums and dish gardens. All it requires is an occasional pinching to keep the plant bushy. Like most pileas, it is easily propagated from stem-tip cuttings.

SILVER-VASE BROMELIAD
(Aechmea fasciata)

ORIGIN: Brazil
FAMILY: Bromeliaceae

**RATING FOR HOME
GROWTH:** Easy

FLOWERING: Dark-blue flowers and rose-colored bract
LIGHT: Filtered light
WATERING: Keep soil on the dry side, but keep cups filled with water
SOIL: Equal parts soil, shredded bark, and sand
PRUNING: None

Here is a truly exotic plant. The leathery, strap-like leaves are green, striped by grayish-white scales and attractive by themselves. However, the amazing part of the silver-vase is its fantastic flower. The actual flowers are dark-blue and short-lived, but the brilliant pink bract can easily last up to 6 months. It's hard to believe that this gorgeous flower is real.

After the flower begins to fade, the silver-vase bromeliad will die. Before it dies, it will produce at least one new plantlet at its base. This offset may be removed by the time it has 4 to 5 leaves and be potted as a new plant. Often a plant will produce more than one offset and each may form a new plant.

The leaves on the silver-vase overlap to produce watertight cups in the center of the plant. It is important to keep these cups filled with water at all times. The soil should be well-drained and kept on the dry side.

VARIEGATED PEPEROMIA
(Peperomia obtusifolia 'Variegata')

ORIGIN: Venezuela
FAMILY: Piperaceae

RATING FOR HOME GROWTH: Easy

FLOWERING: Minute flowers on white spikes.
LIGHT: Filtered light.
WATERING: Keep on the dry side.
SOIL: Equal parts loam, sand and peat moss.
PRUNING: None.

The variegated peperomia is a well-known foliage plant that is most commonly sold in 2¼″ and 3″ pots. It is a slow-growing, compact plant with light green waxy leaves, which are variegated with an off-green and a creamy-white.

The main use for the variegated peperomia has been dish gardens; but, since it will not tolerate too moist condition, it is best to grow the plant in a pot by itself.

Many peperomias are propagated from single leaves, but the variegated peperomia can simply be reproduced from stem-tip cuttings.

WATERMELON PEPEROMIA
(Peperomia sandersii)

ORIGIN: Brazil
FAMILY: Piperaceae

RATING FOR HOME GROWTH: Easy

FLOWERING: Minute flowers on white spikes.
LIGHT: Filtered light.
WATERING: Keep on the dry side.
SOIL: Equal parts loam, sand, and peat moss.
PRUNING: None.

This peperomia in shape, striping, and leaf color actually bears an amazing resemblance to a watermelon. It is this unique feature which attributes to much of the plants popularity.

The watermelon peperomia is not a large plant. It forms a 6″ to 10″ rosette of bluish-green leaves which are striped with bands of silver. The flowers are typical peperomia-type flowers, not showy, but noticeable.

Although easy to grow, this is not a plant for the overzealous waterer. Root and stem rots easily develop under too moist conditions. Propagate your watermelon peperomia from single leaves with patience.

ZEBRA PLANT
(Aphelandra squarrosa)

ORIGIN: Brazil
FAMILY: Acanthaceae

RATING FOR HOME GROWTH: Difficult

FLOWERING: Yellow flowers, with showy golden-yellow bracts.
LIGHT: Filtered light.
WATERING: Keep evenly moist, but not soggy.
SOIL: Equal parts loam, sand, peat moss and leaf mold.
PRUNING: Prune after flowers have faded to keep from getting leggy.

Zebra plants are so attractive that they remain popular despite being so difficult to grow. The shiny dark-green leaves are strikingly veined with white and the golden-yellow bracts remain long after the plant has finished flowering. Because of this spectacular beauty, a zebra plant is worth having even if it only lasts a few months.

The main problem with growng your zebra plant is its need for extremely high humidities. A large terrarium will satisfy this need and is really the only practical way of growing the zebra plant. Another problem is that if this plant is ever allowed to dry out, the bottom leaves will fall off soon afterward.

One good feature about the zebra plant is that it will root easily from stem-tip cuttings. These cuttings can then be grown in a modest size terrarium.

Notes

INDEX
Botanical and common names

A

B